W9-AFU-170

Praise for *Hooked*

There are a lot of people who won't like this book because it explains why sex should occur in appropriate settings, what those settings are, and how scientific evidence today confirms these findings. Modern science is revealing the mysterious workings of the brain as they affect human sexuality, and *Hooked* is a must-read to gain that understanding for every parent, every single person, and anyone contemplating a long-term relationship. It is an invaluable source of information for those who feel we have been given a moral compass, a purpose for our lives, and ability to find the meaning for our lives.

SHEPHERD SMITH
Principal Officer, Institute for Youth Development

Hooked is a timely tool for all concerned about the short- and long-term health of our nation, especially our young people. It provides the needed science and medical perspective to a solution often discounted as a moral, religious, or political issue. Indeed, sex preserved for the context of marriage is still the optimal decision for physical, mental, emotional, social, and spiritual health. Thank you for this excellent work!

LORI KUYKENDALL
Executive Director, Aim for Success

HOOKED

THE BRAIN SCIENCE
ON HOW CASUAL SEX
AFFECTS HUMAN DEVELOPMENT

JOE S. MCILHANEY JR., MD
FREDA MCKISSIC BUSH, MD

NORTHFIELD PUBLISHING

CHICAGO

© 2008, 2019 by
JOE S. MCILHANEY
FREDA MCKISSIC BUSH

All rights reserved. No part of this book may be reproduced in any form without permission in writing from the publisher, except in the case of brief quotations embodied in critical articles or reviews.

Editor: Pamela J. Pugh and Kevin P. Emmert
Interior design: Ragont Design
Cover design: Erik M. Peterson
Cover image of brain copyright © 2018 by Jolygon/Shutterstock (533933176). All rights reserved.
Cover image of male & female icon copyright © 2018 by Topuria Design/Shutterstock (296786381). All rights reserved.

Library of Congress Cataloging-in-Publication Data

Names: Mcilhaney, Joe S., author. | Bush, Freda McKissic.
Title: Hooked : the brain science on how casual sex affects human development
  / Joe S. McIlhaney, Jr., MD, Freda McKissic Bush, MD.
Description: Chicago, IL : Northfield Publishing, [2019] | Earlier edition:
  2008. | Includes bibliographical references and index.
Identifiers: LCCN 2018046573 (print) | LCCN 2018049185 (ebook) | ISBN
  9780802497307 () | ISBN 9780802418357
Subjects: LCSH: Teenagers--Sexual behavior. | Children--Sexual behavior. |
  Adolescent psychology. | Child psychology. | Interpersonal relations in
  adolescence. | Interpersonal relations in children.
Classification: LCC HQ27 (ebook) | LCC HQ27 .M39 2019 (print) | DDC
  306.70835--dc23
LC record available at https://lccn.loc.gov/2018046573

ISBN: 978-0-8024-1835-7

All websites and phone numbers listed herein are accurate at the time of publication but may change in the future or cease to exist. The listing of website references and resources does not imply publisher endorsement of the site's entire contents. Groups and organizations are listed for informational purposes, and listing does not imply publisher endorsement of their activities.

We hope you enjoy this book from Northfield Publishing. Our goal is to provide high-quality, thought-provoking books and products that connect truth to your real needs and challenges. For more information on our other books and products, go to www .moodypublishers.com or write to:

Northfield Publishing
820 N. LaSalle Boulevard
Chicago, IL 60610

3 5 7 9 10 8 6 4 2

Printed in the United States of America

CONTENTS

Introduction   7

   1. Let's Talk Sex   11

   2. Meet the Brain   23

   3. The Developing Brain and Sex   47

   4. Baggage Claim   71

   5. Thinking Long-Term   95

   6. The Pursuit of Happiness   113

   7. Final Thoughts   135

Appendix: Pornography and the Brain   143

Acknowledgments   147

Notes   151

Index   169

INTRODUCTION

One of the most intriguing aspects of the world around us and of our own lives is the subject of sexuality. How do we decide to engage in sex, and how do we select a partner? What does sex do to a relationship? What about sexually transmitted diseases, teen pregnancy, or pornography? How can we understand our own sexual urges, our own hopes for committed relationships and intact families, when we live in a society that sensationalizes sex and encourages us to experiment with it before we have matured enough to find our own identity?

Twenty-eight years ago in 1992, Joe McIlhaney, MD, founded The Medical Institute for Sexual Health to study the science of human sexual behavior and its consequences. For much of its history, the organization has concentrated on the two primary factors that can impair sexual health: nonmarital pregnancy and sexually transmitted infections. But today, with this book, Dr. McIlhaney and coauthor Freda McKissic Bush, MD, provide a deeper understanding of why we make the sexual choices we make and why our children do as well.

In our first edition we showed how modern neuroscience research has uncovered startling new information about how sex affects our brains. The effect of sex on our brains can have all sorts of consequences, including many that scientists are still working to understand. But we do know that sex can literally change a person's brain, influencing the thought process and affecting future decisions. And therein lies both the benefit and the risk. When sex is experienced in healthy ways it adds great value and satisfaction to life, but when experienced in unhealthy ways, at the wrong time, it can damage vital aspects of who we are as human beings.

This book shows the very latest sexual health research and expands our understanding of human behavior. Some of our behavior undermines even our best intentions to be healthy. Thus, this book takes a look at the newest unfolding scientific evidence that can help us understand sexual behavior. This second edition of *Hooked* is more than a mere update of the scientific research that is the foundation of this book. There has been a cultural shift in the sexual norms of our society since the original *Hooked* was published. These cultural changes mandated multiple updates. Armed with new scientific information on sexual behavior and the brain, we can work individually and as a society to bring about a new kind of sexual revolution, one that truly values sexual health.

Is this possible? We earnestly believe so. Consider the changes we have seen just in our lifetimes. It is hard to remember that only a few years ago, people could smoke cigarettes on airplanes, in hospitals, even in doctors' offices. In fact, your doctor may have been smoking as he discussed your diagnosis with you. Today, that is unthinkable!

It is amazing that this cultural change has occurred despite the enormous influence of the tobacco industry and the addiction of millions of men and women to the nicotine in cigarettes. Yet people have learned that smoking is indeed harmful and have chosen in increasing numbers to avoid the consequences: lung cancer, emphysema, heart disease, stroke, and more.

We earnestly believe change for good is possible for the group at greatest risk and highest potential in our society: our young people. The following chapters discuss the development of the adolescent brain and how it is uniquely moldable and receptive to ideas and behaviors. This is especially true with regard to sex—an activity that an adolescent body may be capable of but for which the adolescent mind may not be prepared to think through. This book is designed to speak to parents, teachers, mentors, and young people themselves in plain language and without pretense.

At The Medical Institute for Sexual Health, we endeavor to find scientific truth on issues of sexual health. We want everyone to be fully informed with the most credible scientific information available on issues of sexual behavior and sexual health. We want everyone to be aware of the options that offer the very best chance to have a healthy, successful life; to reach their full potential, free from the repercussions that often accompany poor sexual health decisions.

It is our hope that this book will shed new light on perplexing problems and behaviors. With new insight, perhaps we can not only better understand ourselves and our behavior, but positively impact the emotional and sexual health of the current and future generations.

> FREDA BUSH, MD, CEO
> JOE MCILHANEY, MD Chairman/Founder
> The Medical Institute for Sexual Health
> Austin, Texas

POPULAR CULTURE would have us believe that young people should become involved in sex when they feel ready, and that with proper precautions, everything will be fine. But the facts tell a very different story.

Chapter One

LET'S TALK SEX

SEX!

I t's everywhere. We human beings are made so that even the topic of sex gets our attention. Why? Because, as reliable research indicates, our interest in sex is built into our brains.

And this fascination with sex is absolutely vital. If we did not have this inborn interest in things sexual, we would not have the audacity to overcome our natural hesitation to become very personal with someone else, completely intimate, and literally joined with another.

> "Why not? I wore a condom. She said she wanted to. We're old enough and smart enough to make decisions for ourselves. I'm not a kid anymore."
>
> RYAN, 16

Because of our pervasive interest, society uses sex in many ways. It is one of the constant themes to which persons of all ages are exposed. Sex is used to sell music and clothes to teens, and to sell movies, automobiles, health and fitness equipment, and many other items to adults. This phenomenon has only increased over the years, aided by social media as well as the ever-declining standards in entertainment and public discourse.

Teenagers and young adults are told that there are risks to having sex—namely, that they could contract a sexually transmitted disease or get pregnant. These risks are well known and widely documented. However, teens and adults also know that with the use of condoms or other contraceptive techniques, the morning-after pill, vaccines, careful partner selection, and—truthfully—pure luck, one is less likely to experience these problems. Even though these physical risks are real, are dangerous, and will not be totally eliminated in the foreseeable future, some people are willing to accept or ignore the dangers and plunge into the lifestyle of one partner this year (or today) and another next year (or tomorrow).

But is that all there is to it? Can we really warn young people about these two risks and count on current and future technology to improve their chances of avoiding them? Or are there other risks lying in wait out there—risks of problems that may not be as physically obvious but nevertheless just as devastating to an individual's freedom of opportunity in the future?

The answer is yes. Scientists are now much better able to see and understand what we'll refer to as the third risk.

In the following chapters, we will explore

- various aspects of sexual involvement with another person;
- the results of that behavior on the brain that can last for a lifetime after intimate contact;
- the addictive nature of sex for those involved in a series of short-term hookups or patterns of concurrent relationships leading to unhealthy choices;

- the addictive nature of sex in the context of maintaining a loving marriage;
- the fact that human beings are not slaves to the natural and good physical and emotional desire for sex;
- the fact that our brains allow us to exercise sound judgment;
- how this capacity for good decision making can trump impulse if we practice the habit of letting it do so; and
- a discussion of the burgeoning issue of pornography and its effect on the brain.

AWAKENING

For prepubescent boys and girls, sexual things are asleep. The phrase "sexual awakening" is often used to describe the time in a young person's life when he or she discovers sexual interests. The term "awakening" implies that something was asleep and indeed, for younger children, this is an accurate observation. Little boys' and little girls' bodies look much the same, and they reflect the sexual immaturity of their minds. They may be curious about their own bodies, and the bodies of their parents, or have questions about where babies come from, but they lack the interest and physical development that defines a human being who is equipped for sex and childbearing.

> "He was my first serious boyfriend and I thought I loved him. I really thought if I didn't have sex with him he would leave me. I was fifteen and I'd never had those kinds of feelings for anyone. I can never get that first time back."
>
> **CARRIE, 19**

Puberty is the time of life when boys and girls begin to physically change and develop into adults with sexual desires. The physical changes that define puberty are driven by the sex hormones: estrogen for girls and testosterone for boys. These hormones begin to be produced in increasing quantities, on average, between ages eight and thirteen for girls, and nine and fourteen for boys.[1] These hormones, which are released by the ovaries or testes into the bloodstream, trigger all kinds of fascinating changes. Girls develop breasts, their hips grow wider, and they begin the menstrual cycle. Boys grow taller, their shoulders broaden, and they start growing more hair in various places on their bodies. And puberty, which could be said to be the doorway to adolescence, is the time during which male and female reproductive organs develop to maturity.

But puberty signals far more than a physical change. Mental and emotional transitions accompany the growth and development of the body. Though the changes that puberty produces in the brain can be seen only by neuroscientists, no one who has been around a young person going through this transition doubts that profound mental, emotional, and psychological changes are taking place at this time. These changes include the sudden emergence of physical change and sexual awareness, which can be an emotional roller coaster for any adolescent.

HEALTHY APPETITES

Sex can be considered one of the appetites with which we are born. If you look up "appetite" in Merriam-Webster's Dictionary, you'll read that it's "any of the instinctive desires necessary to keep up organic life." A secondary definition is "an inherent craving." A truth to remember is that appetites are *necessary* but are values-neutral. They can be used appropriately or they can be misunderstood and misused. For example, without an appetite for food, we wouldn't survive. Food provides energy and fuels our bodies. Yet misuse of this natural appetite in the forms of overeating or eating too much of the wrong things can cause cardiovascular disease, diabetes, and many other problems.

These health problems can dramatically change the entire course of an individual's life.

Sex is an important, healthy appetite that fits perfectly the definition of "an instinctive desire necessary to keep up organic life." Without an appetite for sex, there would be no procreation, and human life would come to an end. But as with food, sex can be misunderstood and misused. We can see the physical damage to health from the misuse of sex—HIV/AIDS and sexually transmitted diseases, pornography addiction and nonmarital pregnancy. These are not insignificant problems; they occur far more often than most people realize. And when they do occur, they can change the entire course of a person's life, causing complications they never dreamed of.

In contrast to pregnancy or sexually transmitted disease, the emotional and psychological impact of unwise sexual activity cannot be guarded against with condoms or other forms of contraception. This is a third risk of sex, one that is rarely acknowledged but that has enormous implications for young people and their futures, and for unsuspecting adults. You'll read about it in this book.

> **"I couldn't wait to have sex with her. All my friends were doing it. I was tired of listening to everyone else's stories. I wanted to know what it was like for myself."**
>
> **KEVIN, 17**

SO, WHEN IS IT "SEX"?

So now that we know that sex is a normal appetite, what exactly is it? As strange as it sounds, many people disagree over what sex really is. For example, does penetration have to occur in order for the act to qualify as "sex"? Or can two people "have sex" simply by sexually touching each other, even on top of their clothes? Does oral sex count? What about masturbation? The most reasonable definition suggested by recent brain studies indicates that *sexual activity is any intimate contact between two individuals that involves arousal, stimulation, and/or a response by at least one of the two partners.*

In other words, sexual activity is any intentionally sexually intimate behavior between two partners, or even one person if self-stimulation is used.

However, sexual arousal does not *begin* with the parts of your body that feel the most aroused. Sexual excitement is actually centered in the brain. It is possible to be stimulated and even achieve orgasm without any physical contact with the sexual organs at all. An excellent example of this is a nocturnal emission known as a "wet dream"—when arousal and even ejaculation occurs in dreams during sleep.

> "Sex is when you go all the way with somebody. As long as you don't actually do it, you aren't having sex. So we can still have a good time without worrying about all that other stuff."
>
> MELISSA, 15

Perhaps the best way to describe how sex begins in the brain is to consider a couple and go through the typical sequence of events that leads them to sexual intercourse, assuming the relationship is nonabusive and unselfish. There is usually a progression of physical contact that, sooner or later, acquires the *purpose* of having sexual intercourse. A couple may begin with touching, light kissing, and other behaviors not commonly referred to as sex. This fascinating process is clearly visible with modern brain scan technology, revealing different areas of the brain "lighting up." A couple may not have begun touching with the intention of having sex, but at some point that can become the goal. At that time, the kissing, touching, and any other contact takes on a new energy, and different portions of the brain become engaged and aroused. When those actions are taken with the *intention* of having sex, sexual activity has begun, concluding with physical sexual union.

We can also see from this description why it is necessary to include conduct such as showering together, oral sex, mutual masturbation, and intimate touching as sexual activity.[2] In addition to being included as sexual behavior because of the intent of either or both people involved, these are sexual behaviors because, among other things even short of penetration, they can result in a person becoming infected with a sexually transmitted disease if he or she engages in some of these activities with an infected person.[3] These behaviors are also considered sexual activity since the individuals involved can experience similar emotions of excitement and pleasure as they would from sexual intercourse, as well as experience devastation when the relationship with the person with whom they've engaged in these activities ends.

Integrating all this information leads us to the conclusion that a definition of sexual activity must include not only sexual intercourse, but also anal sex, oral sex, mutual masturbation, showering together, fondling of breasts, other behaviors and, yes, even kissing if done purposely to produce sexual stimulation and gratification.

Sex can and should be a positive experience. It should be the intimate interaction between two persons who care for each other and desire to share their innermost feelings with each other. Sex has many wonderful benefits: the pleasure and satisfaction of becoming an intimate part of another person's body; verbal and physical communication; expressing and deriving pleasure with a partner;

> **"I had no idea how having sex as a teenager could affect the rest of my life. I didn't really know what love was. By the time I got married, sex was so confusing for me. It has been a huge issue in our marriage and I don't know how to fix it."**
>
> **CHRISTIE, 29**

uniting the "two" to become another "one" and, clearly, the potential for procreation.

But sex misused has obvious negative consequences. When one is forced or coerced to have sex, it is not good. When sex is used to accomplish favors or to influence another, it is not good. When sex is used for financial gain, used abusively, or used to humiliate another, it is not good. When sex results in an undesired or unplanned, nonmarital pregnancy or results in a sexually transmitted infection, it is not good. And when sex produces feelings of regret, depression, suicidal ideation, and other emotional problems, it is not good.

NOT JUST A BODY

Now that we have defined sex according to physical activity—according to what our bodies are doing—we're ready to talk about the rest of the story. In order to truly understand why sex sells and why it is so pervasive in our society, we have to understand that humans are not just sex machines or animals. We, as human beings, are so much more.

If we think of sex as only a physical activity to be engaged in at our pleasure, and only for our pleasure, we will be blindsided by problems produced by the misunderstandings and miscalculations of our human nature. If we think our makeup is limited to satisfying appetites, we'll conclude that we can engage in sexual activity, enjoy it on a physical level, and totally disassociate these acts from the rest of what we are as human beings—but we'll be sadly mistaken and be blindsided by what might happen to us.

Going back to the time of sexual awakening, important research into the phenomenon of puberty has yielded some important discoveries. It has been found that teenage boys with high testosterone levels were more likely to engage in sexual behaviors than boys with lower hormone levels.[4] In girls, early puberty has been linked to early age of first sexual intercourse.[5] Yet research has found that parental relationships had the greatest influence on teen sexual behavior.

So what's the point? It is worth remembering that every child's body and brain transforms as he or she gets older, and this transformation has a huge physical and psychological impact on all things sexual. An intense fascination and desire for sex often accompanies these changes. Yet simply going through puberty, or having a sex hormone coursing through a young person's bloodstream, or even a specific genetic disposition, does not determine the decisions they make about sex. Beneficial factors, such as home environment and adult guidance, can help shepherd an adolescent through this tumultuous period in life. Negative guidance, if it dominates, from peers or the media can make the journey much more difficult.

Finally, it is clear that the brain is still developing during puberty, and will continue to do so far after the external physical changes have reached their conclusion.

A 2017 survey of high school adolescents illustrates that sexual activity has more ramifications beyond the physical. The survey showed that both boys and girls who have had sex are more likely to be depressed than their friends who have not. The survey also asked questions regarding the students' considerations of making a suicide attempt, making a suicide plan, and actually attempting suicide. Those students who had not had sexual contact consistently had lower percentages than their sexually experienced classmates on all questions regarding suicide.[6]

In all likelihood, none of these young people were aware that depression and suicidal thoughts might be caused in part by their sexual behavior. Consider the following questions:

- Why are those who were not virgins when they married more likely to divorce than those who remained abstinent until marriage?[7]
- Why are sexually active adolescents more likely to be depressed than their abstaining peers?[8]
- Why do married couples report higher levels of sexual satisfaction than unmarried individuals with multiple sexual partners?[9]

The answers, of course, lie in the fact that human beings are creatures who are much more than physical bodies. We possess the ability for cognitive thought, which includes judgment, abstract thinking, planning for the future, moral intelligence, and other processes that govern our lives. Our decision-making ability, coming from the highest centers of the brain, can guide an individual to the most rewarding sexual behavior—unless bad programming from premature and unwise sexual behavior during the adolescent years has occurred, adversely affecting the brain's ability to make healthy decisions.[10]

This is a risk about which most young people and most parents are totally unaware.

Fortunately, modern neuroscience of the past few years has opened a door of understanding that provides incredibly helpful guidance away from trouble. Many of the answers to the questions above, and others, may be found in modern neuroscientific research, the study of the human brain and nervous system, which has revealed startling new information about how sex affects the brain.

In the past, efforts to accurately assess the connection between sex, love, sexual desire, sexual risk-taking, and so on with brain activity were limited. But with the aid of modern research techniques and technologies, scientists are confirming that sex is more than a momentary physical act. It produces powerful, even lifelong, changes in our brains that direct and influence our future to a surprising degree.[11] This new neuroscience information, which has greatly expanded over the past three decades, has transformed the scientific discussion about sex. Perspectives from medical, public health, and social science literature will also be utilized in this book to enhance our understanding of sexual behavior in adolescents and young adults in the larger cultural context.

The uniqueness of becoming an intimate part of another person's mind and body—emotional and physical bonding, both experienced in a healthy way, and the vital role this plays in one's health, happiness, and hope for the future—is the central issue we will be explaining in this book. It is probably the most important outcome of healthy, positive sex.

TO **THINK** ABOUT

- How can "sexual activity" be defined? How do the authors arrive at this description?
- When is sex a positive experience? When is it not?
- How are humans more than a collection of physical body parts?

Chapter Two

MEET THE BRAIN

Some individuals have been disappointed to find that as they move from one sexual partner to another, they not only are *not finding ultimate pleasure but are feeling worse about themselves and their many sexual partners.*[1] In fact, studies show that those in casual relationships find that these sexual patterns often prevent such relationships from blossoming into romance.[2] They wonder why they feel this way.

At the same time, for a married couple, sex is often spoken of as the deepest level of communication. It is seen and felt as a bonding experience by them and central to a healthy relationship.[3] Indeed, married couples have sex more often than single sexually active people.[4] What is going on? How can this be? Can sex be a healthy, relationship-building

> **"After we began having sex I felt dead inside a lot. I almost felt like I was invisible, except when we would have sex. Then I would feel alive for those few minutes. I would crave sex for that feeling."**
>
> **JENNIFER, 19**

experience for married couples, but only a physical encounter for single people just "hooking up"?

THE BRAIN: A SEX ORGAN?

Until recently, scientists, psychologists, and physicians had little in the way of research and data to connect the dots. They knew instinctively, just as countless generations of sexually experienced people did, that sex is more than just a physical experience. They knew it engaged the mind in powerful, if largely unknown, ways. But they had no way of really knowing what was happening in the brain when people experienced love, passion, lust, sex, or other emotions and activities.

Today, however, thanks to breakthroughs in neuroscience research techniques, scientists have been able to literally view the activity of the brain as it functions. With state-of-the-art mapping and imaging tools, researchers have unlocked a new world of data on what happens between your ears each day.[5]

In addition, new methods of tracking brain chemicals have allowed scientists to understand when and how much of these chemicals are released and how they influence behavior. We now have scientific studies about brain function and sexual thoughts and behavior that are not only fascinating but also true breakthroughs in our understanding of ourselves and the intriguing part of our behavior called sex.[6] And yes, this science does establish once and for all that more happens during sex than physical activity or the transfer of secretions (or germs or sperm). What we now know from science is what some have been saying for years—that the largest and most important sex organ is the brain. To understand this, we'll need a basic understanding of the brain.

BRAIN BASICS

The appearance of the outside of the brain is familiar to most people. Seen in biology classrooms and in textbooks, the familiar gray lump is easily identifiable. Many have learned about the main parts of the brain and know that different parts control different functions. But most of us don't consciously consider how this complex organ functions in our daily lives.

In many ways, this is a good thing. For example, we don't have to figure out how to walk, breathe, swallow, or any number of the things we do every day, almost automatically. We don't have to stop and think how to do these things.

However, for our understanding of how we think and of our decisions about behavior, it can be exceedingly helpful to understand the internal workings of our brains and the brains of our children.

Neurons: The *neuron* is the primary cell of the brain. It is the cell through which the electricity flows that makes the brain work. A neuron consists of a cell body containing the nucleus and the surrounding fluid called the cytoplasm, which fills the neuron cell like water in a balloon. The most explicit image of the neuron is one that includes many, sometimes thousands, short projections (dendrites) from the nerve cell for receiving transmissions, and one long projection (an axon) for sending transmissions.

Support Cells: By the time a person reaches the end of her adolescent years, her brain contains more than 10 billion neurons. In addition, the brain holds another 100 billion *support cells.* These cells hold the neurons together, assist in the growth and development of the neurons, and remove waste material when a neuron dies. The brain is richly supplied with blood vessels, a part of the support cell system.

Synapses: In order for the brain to function, the various neurons need to be able to communicate with one another and connect into a cohesive whole. Much like the internet for computers, the brain's network requires connections and continuity—otherwise it would simply be a collection of dead ends. The connections that bridge the gaps between neurons are called *synapses*. The neurons in question are not seamlessly physically connected by the synapses; there is always a small gap where the electricity is carried by a neurochemical, which will be discussed later in this chapter.

Synapses are organic connections that rely on use for their very existence. In this manner, they are somewhat like your muscles and other kinds of organic tissue; they need exercise. In other words, use them or lose them.

When a new activity or experience or thought occurs, it can result in a strengthening of the connection between neurons, or even in a new connection altogether. These connections are critical for memory, behavior, emotions, desires, and any number of other outcomes that activity or experience brings. If that experience or activity occurs again, the connection is used and strengthened in the process. If that connection is not used, the synapse can weaken and perhaps even die. This process refers to either a continued connection between neurons or to weakening or even a loss of connection—not the life or death of the neurons themselves, although that can and does occur as well.[7]

Neurons are tiny. About 30,000 fit on the head of a pin. Yet if the neurons in just one human brain (about 100 billion) were placed end to end, they would circle the earth four times.[8] The synaptic connections are even greater, with a total of more than 100 trillion (10^{14}).[9] The human brain is, without question, the most complicated three-pound mass of matter in the known universe.

THE MOLDABLE BRAIN

A fundamental fact about the brain is that from before birth until death, the brain is moldable and adaptable.[10] It is not a rigid, immutable structure, but an organ that can grow and mold. Please remember this concept as you read the rest of this book. It is a foundational understanding of almost all we say from this point on. And remember that one's brain can mold because of behavior or experience today, and remold because of subsequent and different experience later—though that remolding can at times be very difficult to accomplish.

The primary things that change in the brain structure, that mold it, are its synapses. Synapses are either sustained or allowed to weaken or deteriorate based on behavior and experience. It may seem incredible, but the things we see, do, and experience actually cause part of our brains to flourish (i.e., synapses that survive and strengthen) and part of our brain to weaken (i.e., synapses that weaken, disintegrate, or die).[11]

For example, how many of us remember the names of our kindergarten classmates? Perhaps if you continued in school with some of them for several years, your brain would retain the information. But for most of us, the information would not be useful and the synaptic connections would be pruned to make way for more pertinent information, as we forget the names of those long-ago classmates.

Another example that graphically illustrates the way our experience and behavior mold our brains is shown by brain imaging of violinists. Such pictures of professional violinists show that the portion of the brain that controls the fingers on their left hand (the hand that fingers the violin strings) are much larger than the same area of the brains of individuals who are not violinists.[12]

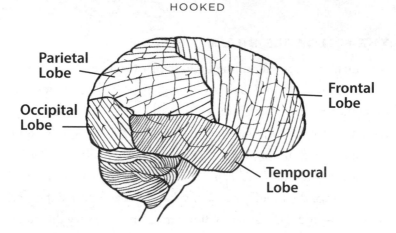

The brain and its lobes within the cerebral cortex.

In these examples, it is clear that the connections (synapses) in the human brain

- are adaptable and subject to change, and
- have enormous implications for human behavior and actions.

NEUROCHEMICALS

As we have seen, the brain would not work without neurons, support cells, or synapses. There is a fourth absolutely essential part of the brain—neurochemicals.

A neurochemical is one that is unique to or active in the brain. There are hundreds of these chemicals bathing the brain cells, synapses, and support cells all the time. Some of these chemicals are necessary for messages to go from one cell, across the synapse, to another cell. Without these chemicals, most messages could not move through the brain at all.

It is important to remember that these neurochemicals are values-neutral; they produce emotional responses and changes in the brain whenever they are released. The effect is the same whether the situation or behavior that triggered the release is healthy or unhealthy. Thus, the brain can be molded to reinforce healthy behaviors, but also unhealthy ones, depending on experiences.

In addition to the neurochemicals necessary for moving messages along, there are other neurochemicals that play amazing, exciting, and almost unbelievable roles in our thinking, desires, and behavior.

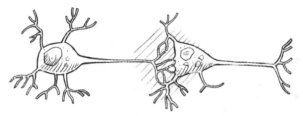

The neural circuit. This includes the neuron's cell body, the axon extending from one neuron to another, and the synapse, or connection point between two neurons in the brain. The synapse is the functional connection point between two neurons.

Dopamine: The messenger chemical (neurotransmitter) *dopamine* can make a person feel good when he or she does something exciting or rewarding. Dopamine, therefore, has great influence over human behavior. The commonly used term for what dopamine does is "reward signal"—that is, when we do something exciting, dopamine rewards us by flooding our brains and making the brain cells produce a feeling of excitement or of well-being.

Dopamine can make us feel good because of the intense energy, exhilaration, and focused attention it produces when we do something important or stimulating. It makes us feel the need or desire to repeat pleasurable, exciting, and rewarding acts. It is even said by some neuroscientists that when we are craving pleasurable experiences, we are actually craving more dopamine. They even say that since learning is dependent on this "excitation," that dopamine is the driving force in our brains.[13]

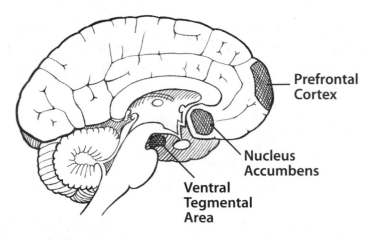

— Prefrontal Cortex

Nucleus Accumbens

Ventral Tegmental Area

Areas of the brain that are involved with the production and transmission of dopamine. Dopamine is involved in "rewarding" the brain for risky or exhilarating behavior. This might include positive things such as good grades or negative things such as driving too fast.

We can see, therefore, that dopamine is vital to living a healthy, normal life. Dopamine gives us a charge of excitement and rewards us for having the courage to take an action with an uncertain outcome. It can, for example, reward someone for taking the risk of choosing to get married, have a child, start a new job or business, or other significant venture. We humans are not—and shouldn't be—averse to taking risks.

Dopamine plays a particularly powerful role in the lives and brains of adolescents. Dopamine levels reach their peak in late childhood. But dopamine levels continue to increase in one important part of the brain, the prefrontal cortex. This is the final portion of the brain to complete its development, and it is the part of the brain responsible for the mature decision making available in adulthood.[14]

Because adolescence is such a dynamic time of life change, dopamine plays an especially important role for young people during this time. Consider, for example, a vital and natural, yet highly risky move for an adolescent—separating from parents to become a self-sustaining adult. Dopamine rewards the young adult for this risky venture by making him feel excited and good about achieving independence even if he does not know if he can, in fact, provide for himself.

This same risk/reward holds true for picking a lifelong mate: "What if I'm not marrying the right person?" Or having a child: "Can we afford a child? Will we be good parents? What if our child has special challenges?" Countless fears that could stymie a person are overcome by dopamine, which brings excitement to these new ventures.[15]

Dopamine is clearly one of the most important messenger chemicals in the brain. As we are seeing, it has many functions, including important roles in behavior, cognition, motor activity, and motivation and reward. Through its unique impact on the brain, dopamine helps guide human behavior. It should be noted, however, that dopamine is values-neutral. In other words, it is an involuntary response that cannot tell right from wrong, or beneficial from harmful. It can reward all kinds of behavior without distinction.

Examples of harmful dopamine rewards are the use of nonprescriptive drugs, nonmarital sexual involvement, or activities such as the viewing of pornography, excessive drinking, dangerous thrill-seeking, and so on. The "high" that these behaviors can produce can cause an adolescent (and an adult) to want to seek more of that good feeling. To reproduce the good feeling, they seek to repeat the behavior. Their desire for the exciting feeling can overwhelm their ability to accurately calculate the risk of the behavior—or for that matter even worry about it, if they do consider the risk.[16]

An even more subtle danger regarding addictive drugs and other dangerous stimuli is that most of them can overstimulate the dopamine neurons and cause the brain to become relatively resistant to dopamine, thus causing the individual to seek more of the drug or of the behavior that produced the good feelings in the first place. This of course can be part of the reason why addiction to drugs or to certain behaviors occurs.

Almost all addictive drugs—including alcohol, cocaine, heroin, amphetamines, and even marijuana and nicotine—increase dopamine reward signals.[17]

The danger, of course, is that if young people have been receiving a dopamine reward of good feelings from dangerous behavior such as driving too fast, smoking, sex, and others, they can feel compelled to increase that behavior in order to achieve the same good feeling.[18]

There is more risk than might seem apparent from this statement. We'll go into more depth later, but remember that the brain is a moldable organ. Consider, for example, the heady experience of driving very fast. It is exciting; it triggers a values-neutral dopamine reward and strengthens the synapses that lead to making habitually unsafe driving decisions.

When this brain molding occurs as a result of the experience of driving fast, the individual can become immune to a more mature understanding that driving fast is unwise and dangerous. He or she might accept "driving fast" as normal and live life based on that assumption.[19] This same scenario can play out with alcohol, drugs, violence, or almost any other human activity.

Sex is one of the strongest generators of the dopamine reward.[20] For this reason, young people particularly are vulnerable to falling into a cycle of dopamine reward for potentially damaging sexual behavior. They can get hooked on it.

But the beneficial effect of dopamine for the married couple is that sex may play a role in "addicting" them to each other and thus reinforcing their desire to remain together year after year.

Oxytocin: Another neurochemical that is critically important to healthy sex and bonding is oxytocin. While it is present in both genders, it is primarily active in females. According to the research we have today, the female body uses oxytocin in reproduction, bonding, and social behavior. The body uses it both as a hormone circulating in the blood and as a neurotransmitter in the brain.[21]

These actions of oxytocin seem at first to be arbitrary and disconnected. But look again. They all have to do with reproduction, and the nourishment of and provision for a supportive and protective environment for a marriage and then for any children that may join the couple.

REASON FOR OXYTOCIN RELEASE:	ACTION OF OXYTOCIN:
Meaningful or intimate touching with another individual	Bonding and trust in the other person
Sexual intercourse	Bonding and trust in the other person
Onset of labor in a pregnant woman	Oxytocin causes uterine contractions in association with other mechanisms, results in birth
Nipple stimulation after delivery of an infant	Helps produce the flow of milk from a mother's breast during nursing

One of the requirements for the continuation of the human race is that men and women desire to have sexual intercourse with each other. The act of intercourse results not only in a bonding (and resulting brain molding) of the two people, but often produces children. When the parents are truly committed and bonded together, the odds are much better that the baby will be born into a home with two parents who stay together to raise him. Oxytocin is intimately involved in all these steps. We could almost call oxytocin the neurohormone of life itself. One dramatic example of the strong bonding effect of oxytocin on the mother-infant relationship occurs during breastfeeding. As a mother holds her baby skin-to-skin and nurses, her brain is flooded with oxytocin. The presence of oxytocin produces a chemical impact on the mother's brain, molding it to make her want to be with her baby and willing to inconvenience herself for her baby. Oxytocin is intimately involved in the bonding process between a mother and child. In the extreme circumstance of a mother giving her life for her baby, she is willing to do so not just because the child is "cute," but because her brain is molded and "bound" to that baby. The bonding effect that oxytocin initiates is indeed powerful.[22] And, of course, oxytocin is the chemical in a woman's body that causes the milk let down that then provides the life-giving nourishment for the new baby.

This oxytocin impact is obviously vital for the survival of human infants since they are totally unable to provide for themselves in the early years of their lives. However, without oxytocin, babies might not be conceived at all. Here is where the research about oxytocin becomes even more interesting. When two people touch each other in a warm, meaningful, and intimate way, oxytocin is released into the woman's brain. The oxytocin then does two things: increases a woman's desire for more touches and can begin producing bonding of the woman to the man she has been spending time in physical contact with, as her brain begins to be molded to connect her to the man.

This desire for more touch and the bonding that develops between a man and a woman often lead to the most intimate of physical contact—sexual intercourse. With sexual intercourse and orgasm, the woman's brain is flooded with oxytocin, causing her to desire this same kind of contact again and again with this man she has bonded to, producing even stronger bonding, as their brains are more significantly molded to connect them together.[23]

But there is more. The oxytocin bonding that takes place in the normal male-female relationship often can result in long-term connectedness. For example, in America, when a marriage is intact, it is rare for a woman to have sexual intercourse with anyone except her husband.[24] This remarkable stability is undoubtedly in part a result of the effect of oxytocin and brain molding. And the significance of this is that the brain molding initiated by oxytocin results in the bonding of a mother and father (part of the reason marriages often last for many years), greatly increasing the chance for a child to be raised in a nurturing two-parent home, which studies have shown provides a child the most advantageous environment for growing into his or her potential.[25]

The important thing to recognize is that the desire to connect is not *just* an emotional feeling. Bonding is real because it has become a part of the way one's brain is molded—a powerful connection that often cannot be undone without great emotional pain.[26] Real brain chemicals act on real brain cells, causing those brain cells to mold and to bind individuals together. While no one can prove exactly why the brain was made to respond to the initial oxytocin effect in this way, some valid observations as to why it is important are easy to make. Simply put, the continuation of the human race has always depended on men and women forming relationships, conceiving and bearing children, and raising those children together until they can care for themselves . . . and continue the cycle.

More and more scientists and behavioral experts are connecting the dots and concluding that oxytocin not only is key to initiating the bonding of a mother and child, but also produces a like effect between a mother and father.[27] Just as nature has provided a mechanism that works to keep sexually active married couples together, so it has in this way provided a built-in mechanism to ensure that infants are not abandoned.

As mentioned earlier, neurohormones including oxytocin are values-neutral. Much like dopamine, it is an involuntary process that cannot distinguish between a one-night stand and a lifelong soul mate. Oxytocin can cause a woman to begin to bond to a man even during what was expected to be a short-term sexual relationship. She may know he is not the man she would want to marry but intimate sexual involvement may cause her to be so attached to him she can't make herself separate. This can lead to a woman being taken off-guard by a desire to stay with a man she would otherwise find undesirable and staying with him even if he is possessive or abusive.

Finally, an important finding of scientists about oxytocin is that it can produce a feeling of trust in a person with whom a female is in close contact. When a woman considers engaging in sex with a man, she needs to be able to trust him. A woman who is being approached sexually by a man is very vulnerable. He is almost always stronger than she is. He could do things to her physically that she does not want. He can infect her with an STD. He also can cause her to become pregnant. If she does become pregnant and has a baby, she has to trust the man to stay with her and not leave. Then she needs to trust that he will help provide food, clothing, and shelter for her and the child. Finally, she needs to trust that he will provide love and connectedness for her and the child.

On being approached by a man for sex or for marriage, she may not think this far into the future or consider adverse consequences to her actions, but her trust in the man is fundamental to her joining her body to his or even joining her future to his in marriage. Oxytocin helps build this trust that is so essential to a healthy relationship.

There is a warning here for parents and young people, particularly young women. If a young woman becomes physically close to and hugs a man, it will trigger the bonding process, creating a greater desire to be near him and, most significantly, place greater trust in him. Then, if he wants to escalate the physical nature of the relationship, it will become harder and harder for her to say no.[28] The adolescent girl who enters into a close physical relationship may, therefore, find herself, because of the normal effect of her brain hormones and the brain molding that results, desiring more physical contact and trusting a male who may be using manipulative pledges of love and care only to get her to have sex with him.

Louann Brizendine, MD, a neuropsychiatrist at the University of California, offers compelling evidence of how quickly this process can be initiated:

From an experiment on hugging, we also know that oxytocin is naturally released in the brain after a twenty-second hug from a partner—sealing the bond between the huggers and triggering the brain's trust circuits. So don't let a guy hug you unless you plan to trust him. Touching, gazing, positive emotional interaction, kissing, and sexual orgasm also release oxytocin in the female brain. Such contact may just help flip the switch on the brain's romantic love circuits.[29]

In addition, unless they are guided by parents or other caring adults, they cannot know that the cascade of physical contact that initiates an outpouring of oxytocin—then resulting in brain molding—can cause a girl to accept short-term sexual relations as normal, a brain pattern that can imperil a future marriage relationship. Fortunately, the brain is moldable for life. Oxytocin is continually secreted with intimate encounters for life. That means that future marriage relationships can become healthy. So, all is not lost. Still, studies clearly show that if a person has had sex before marriage, they are more likely to divorce when they do marry. Perhaps this is a result of unhealthy brain molding from past relationships that can require intentional effort to re-mold, such as undergoing counseling, spiritual commitment, and so on.

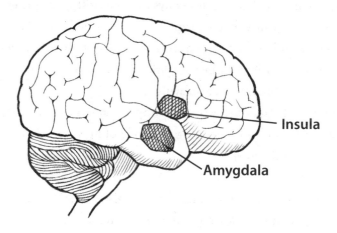

Areas within a woman's brain believed to be involved in the development of trust and trustworthiness. The brain chemical oxytocin likely plays an important role in these processes and is involved in maternal care, social attachment, and bonding. Perception of another person's face is associated with an emotional response within the amygdala. The insula helps translate this emotional response into a feeling about the person.

While the hormonal effect of oxytocin is ideal for marriage, it can cause problems for the unmarried woman or girl who is approached by a man desiring sex. Once again, the warning is that a woman's brain can cause her to be blindsided by a bad relationship that she thought was good because of the physical contact, the oxytocin response, and the brain molding that the sexual behavior generates. The truth about such a relationship may be apparent to parents or friends who are concerned about the girl's well-being, but it takes wisdom and tact to effectively warn a young woman about a relationship that others can see could be dangerous to her.

Not all relationships, of course, are made up of a manipulative male and an unaware female, and our point is not to imply this. But young women especially need to be aware of the powerful effect of oxytocin. When a couple is involved in even a short-term relationship and breaks up and then each moves on to a new sexual partner, they are breaking an oxytocin bond—and perhaps even a brain-molding bond—that has formed. This severing of the bond can help explain the incredibly painful emotions that sexually active people often feel when they break up.[30]

In addition, they cannot know that such short-term sexual relationships may have molded their brain in such a way that it may be more difficult in the future to have a healthy bonded marriage that is a stable relationship and provides a healthy nest for children that might be conceived and born into their home, a problem we'll discuss later. To be sure, such marriage-threatening brain molding can be overcome, but may require lots of commitment and work— something we'll discuss later.

Vasopressin: Women are not the only ones who bond during intimate physical contact. The neurochemical involved in the male brain response and synaptic change is called *vasopressin*. It plays a role in many body functions such as blood pressure regulation and, through its influence on kidney function, fluid regulation in the body. Vasopressin seems to have two primary functions related to relationships: initiation of bonding of the man to his mate and attachment to his offspring.[31]

Due to the remarkable structural similarity between oxytocin and vasopressin, it should come as no surprise that these two neurochemicals share similar activity. Often referred to as the "monogamy molecule," vasopressin seems to be a primary cause of men attaching to women with whom they have close and intimate physical contact. Human studies on vasopressin in regard to social cognition are currently underway.[32] Though vasopressin has not been studied as much as has oxytocin, we know it plays an important role in initiating sexual bonding and bonding between fathers and children. As with oxytocin, this mechanism is extremely important for the proper care of children. In the words of one researcher, "the presence of the father and the display of paternal behavior have been shown to facilitate the physical and behavioral development of offspring."[33] Therefore, just as with oxytocin, vasopressin is vitally important to our survival as a race.

Just like dopamine and oxytocin, vasopressin is values-neutral. If a male enters into a physical relationship with a female unwisely, he could bond to her. This bonding could lead to brain molding leading to a long-term relationship that is unhealthy and destructive because it was an unwise relationship to start with, yet the brain keeps the couple together, even if the couple is in an unhealthy relationship.

As with dopamine and oxytocin, vasopressin has a powerful impact on human behavior. Yet most people are totally unaware of this. Men may question why they keep going back to a woman who treats them poorly or may wonder why they never seem able to feel, deep inside, a commitment to a woman after having sex partner after sex partner. Sadly, they simply do not know that their brains are flooded with vasopressin during sexual intercourse and that this neurochemical produces a brain change and a partial bond with every woman they have sex with. They do not realize that this pattern of having sex with one woman and then breaking up and then having sex with another woman limits them to experience only one form of brain activity common to humans involved sexually— the dopamine rush of sex.[34] The resulting brain molding says to the man, "This is normal." The individual who goes from sex partner to sex partner is causing his brain to mold and gel so that it eventually begins accepting that sexual pattern as normal. For most people, this brain pattern seems to interfere with the development of the neurological circuits necessary for the long-term relationships that for most people result in stable marriages and family development. The pattern of changing sex partners, therefore, seems to decrease their ability to form a committed relationship.[35]

As we have said, the inability to bond after multiple liaisons is rooted in the fact that our behaviors actually physically change our brains. The pattern of hooking up and breaking up and hooking up again can eventually override the natural bonding that occurs between two intimately involved individuals. Although oxytocin, vasopressin, and dopamine continue to be released with sexual intimacy, the physical rut that is formed between the synapses subconsciously influences the continuation of the promiscuous behavior. The conflict between the natural bonding and the learned behavior can result, in some cases, in a boredom with sex itself. Mark Regnerus and Jeremy Uecker sum it up well: "People who enter a casual sex relationship to not be complicated and hurt often get complication and hurt."[36]

41

SCENT SENSE: PHEROMONES

Pheromones are chemical signals secreted by the skin and sweat glands of many animals, including mammals. Most pheromones act through the sense of smell, even when the smell is not consciously detected, and most illicit a response that is not a "learned response." They have been known to be involved in attraction of the sexes, mate choice, and interactions between parents and offspring.[37]

Scientists are still debating the role of pheromones in humans. The latest reviews of previous human pheromone studies indicate that the studies are weak and call for more controlled studies.[38] Though studies on the impact of pheromones on sexual attraction in humans is difficult, there are situations in which it would seem important to establish some understanding. For example, in situations requiring close confinement of men and women, such as on military ships, the question arises whether pheromones result in sexual attraction that is subconscious but results in sexual connecting between men and women. Such scenarios show the practical need of further pheromone human research.

Pheromones obviously do not overwhelm all other factors that influence sexual behavior choices. They are, however, one more piece of evidence in the case we are building that unconscious, powerful influences are at work regarding sexual behavior choices. Most of us think of our choices as being influenced by some kind of love or emotional feeling. Instead, it can be strongly influenced by these neurohormones we have been discussing, including perhaps the strange chemical pheromone.

We have discussed several major hormones and neurohormones that influence the brain's learning behavior and sexual interest. There are many other chemicals that also play roles here, including endorphins, estrogen, progesterone, testosterone, and serotonin. While understanding the roles these hormones play is helpful, a discussion here would distract from the point of this chapter.

MORE THAN A FEELING

It has often been said that a human's largest sexual organ is the brain. It is certainly the most complicated, and it is responsible for activities and effects that go far beyond the momentary pleasure of sex.

We've seen how the brain is composed of multiple neurons, all of which are connected by synapses. These synapses can be created, grow, or deteriorate based on our thoughts and actions. In this manner, each person actually changes the very structure of the brain with the choices he or she makes and the behavior he or she is involved in.

We've also seen how our choices are affected by chemicals in our brains. These chemicals are in place for important reasons, and have much to do with the survival of the human race. Dopamine floods our brains and rewards us for exciting or risky behavior—like growing up and separating from our parents, committing to another person in marriage, or birthing and raising children. Oxytocin helps females become attached to men, have children, nurse those children as they initiate milk let-down, and bond with those children, thus giving them the greatest chance for a healthy future. In like manner, vasopressin helps men become attached to a woman and to their children. As a recent study of the brain's involvement in love and "mating" says, "both oxytocin and vasopressin have been shown to be crucially involved in romantic love and bonding." These researchers made this statement in the context of their studies that showed that one of the brain centers called the nucleus accumbens is associated with other brain centers rich in dopamine and oxytocin receptors, which play a central role in emotions of romantic love and a desire for "union" with another.[39] This research is supported by the findings of Regnerus and Uecker, as pointed out in their book *Premarital Sex in America*, when they make these statements:

> Indeed, the sex is operating as it tends to—bonding persons, deepening relationships, and fostering greater interpersonal intimacy.
>
> The hormone oxytocin is released during orgasm in both sexes: inside the brain, oxytocin is involved in social recognition and bonding, and it may also contribute to the formation of trust between people.
>
> Mutually pleasurable sexual relationships generate more orgasms, more oxytocin, and more bonding sentiments, intentions, and emotions.[40]

Taken as a whole, these complicated processes offer a compelling pattern. They are designed to lead toward and strengthen long-term monogamous relationships, supporting and reinforcing the family structure that is so vital to our survival.

However, we have also seen that these chemicals and processes are values-neutral. They can produce unconsciously motivated responses that result in all kinds of behavior, including activities that are dangerous or unwise. It is important to note that the brain does not run out of oxytocin or vasopressin or any of the neurochemicals—and there will be no shortage of these chemicals when one enters marriage. As far as we can tell, they will always be produced with the stimulation we have shown here. The problem is the activity may have produced brain wiring or molding that then affects one's future decisions, emotions, and behavior.

The brain, then, is very involved in our decisions about sex and the actions that follow, far beyond what is apparent on the surface. We know that nonmarital sexual activity can produce sexually transmitted infection and unplanned pregnancy, but it is just as clear that some of the most powerful effects of sex are emotional and psychological. Next, we'll see what this means for young people whose brains and bodies are still growing and developing.

TO THINK ABOUT

- What do the authors mean by "use them or lose them," referring to synapses? What do synapses have to do with the brain being moldable?
- What does it mean to call dopamine and other neurochemicals "values-neutral"?
- How are oxytocin and vasopressin bonding chemicals?

Chapter Three

THE DEVELOPING BRAIN AND SEX

We have already gotten a glimpse of how the three-pound human brain is the most complex mass of matter in the universe. But just how does the brain develop? Can anything influence brain development for better or for worse? And how does the topic of sex fit into this discussion?

We all are familiar with the external signs of physical growth as a person goes from baby-hood through childhood and adolescence: loose teeth, shoes that don't fit anymore, clumsi-ness, and a voracious appetite, just to name a few. But how does the growth process affect the brain? After all, just as the rest of the body does, the human brain itself grows and develops from birth to adult-hood. The maturation of the brain is in many ways more delicate,

> "I've seen the changes in some of my friends. I've seen them cry and feel bad and lose hope that they will ever be loved. I haven't found the love of my life yet either, but I am so glad I don't have the baggage they do."
>
> CHERYL, 26

more unpredictable, more important, and, until recently, less understood than that of any other part of the body.

For many parents of adolescents, the phenomenon of the developing brain can be summarized in a single question: "Why in the world does my teenager act this way?" Historically, the scientific community was not able to respond to that question very well. In the past, most of the techniques for studying the adolescent brain were invasive or potentially damaging. Therefore, little was known about the activity going on inside a young person's brain.[1]

INSIDE THE ADOLESCENT BRAIN

During the past twenty-five years, scientists have been able to use new technologies such as MRI (Magnetic Resonance Imaging), fMRI (functional MRI), and PET (positron emission tomography) scans to study the brain in groundbreaking new ways. The technology called MRI, which relies on magnets instead of X-rays, has revealed amazing new information about adolescent brain activity. Since magnets do not hurt living tissue

> "I want to protect my kids. I would never want them to go through what I did, and have to live with the guilt and regret. I wouldn't wish it on anybody, least of all them."
>
> MARK, 36

and, therefore, can be used over and over with young people as their brains grow through the years, this technology can be used to observe adolescent brains as they grow and develop.

A *functional MRI* uses similar technology to observe how much oxygen a given portion of the brain is using. When an area of the brain is "working," it must have oxygen to fuel that work. That increased oxygen consumption is measured by functional MRI, revealing new data about what area of the brain is "working."

A *PET scan* is a medical imaging technique that produces a three-dimensional image or map of the brain by measuring the flow of blood to any given area. When an area of the brain is active, there is more blood flow, and the PET scanner can "see" that. One disadvantage of the *PET* scan is that a "tracer" must be infused into the subject being studied. For this reason, we more often find the *functional MRI* used in research.[2]

Primarily with the aid of MRI, scientists have made an important discovery about the brain's growth and maturation. The part of the brain that controls the ability to make fully mature judgment decisions is not physically mature until an individual reaches his or her midtwenties. In other words, the part of a brain that is responsible for complex assessments about future consequences and responsibility is still growing throughout the teen years and into the midtwenties.[3]

Most of us give little thought to where our decision-making ability comes from. To many, it seems to be an extension of our personalities and opinions. Simply put, we rarely think about *how* we think. Through studies of individuals who have either experienced brain trauma or undergone surgery on different portions of their brain, neuroscientists have known for years that our capacity for cognitive thought comes primarily from what is called the prefrontal cortex of the brain's frontal lobes.[4] It is located at the front of the brain, behind the forehead.

This area is the source of thought that is responsible for setting priorities, organizing plans and ideas, forming strategies, controlling impulses, and allocating attention.[5] This type of thinking is called "cognitive," which also includes initiating appropriate and moral behavior, anticipating how behavior today can affect one's future, and sound judgment decisions. The adolescent years are critical for developing these functions. While young people can make some good judgment calls for themselves, it is impossible for them to always make fully mature judgment decisions until their midtwenties, when their brains are finally mature.[6]

One of the best and most understandable evidences of this observation is that car rental companies will not rent their cars to a person under the age of twenty-five unless special arrangements have been made or a higher rate is charged. The reason given by these companies is that the risk of damage and destruction of their property is excessive when driven by younger drivers, regardless of education or employment.

The finding, therefore, that cognitive maturity does not reach completion until the midtwenties does not mean that young people are somehow mentally slow or that they do not possess the capacity for complex thought. It does mean that their brains are not fully physically equipped to make sound judgments and reason through long-term consequences of behavior they might become involved in until a little later in life. When people first hear this information, they often take it to mean that young people are inherently less intelligent than adults. This is a misinterpretation; young people can be extremely intelligent. For example, Mozart completed many compositions before the age of fourteen. Picasso painted the *Picador* at age eight. Many other examples of people demonstrating intelligence and giftedness at a young age abound. Also, it does not mean that young people are not otherwise physically mature. LeBron James went directly from high school basketball to the NBA at age nineteen; he was a more physically gifted basketball player than many who were years older and far more experienced.

The ability to make sound judgments, then, does not depend on one's intelligence.

What we now know about development of this part of the brain—the prefrontal cortex—is that during the explosive period of adolescent brain development, synapses (the connections that bridge the gaps between neurons) play an integral part in forming the mature brain. Research has shown that there are two periods in one's life during which there is an explosive proliferation of connections between brain cells—during the last few weeks before birth and just before puberty. The brain manufactures far more of these connections (synapses) than are necessary. The interesting thing we now know about this excess of synapses is that some are meant to be strengthened and some are meant to die. It just depends on what we experience.[7] As we have already seen, synapses that strengthen and proliferate are those that are used (think of "use them or lose them"). The synapses that are not used usually weaken or die.[8]

SETTING THE COURSE

Adolescent brains can often be positively molded by structure, guidance, and discipline provided by caring parents and other adults. This may include any number of positive inputs including loving, caring guidance, discipline (sometimes unpleasant but not dangerous), and also behavior in which the teen is required to take a chance because the outcome is unpredictable: trying out for the high school football team, learning to drive, going to college. These all carry

> **"I wish I had said no. I wish I had been strong enough, and I wish my parents had helped me more. I had no idea that having sex would change my life so much."**
>
> **KAREN, 20**

51

certain emotional or even physical risks, but are necessary in order for the young person to separate from parents and grow into an independent individual.

Adolescent brains can also be negatively molded by unstructured experiences or bad input such as neglect, poor guidance, poor structure, or lack of discipline. For these unfortunate youth, this means that the guidance they receive and experiences they have had may have come from the media, pop culture, or peers who are as neglected, immature, and as poorly guided as they are.

What is certain is that the adolescent brain will be molded by one or the other.[9]

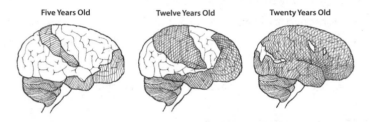

The prefrontal cortex of the brain is not mature until a person grows out of adolescence and into their midtwenties. Shaded portions represent the growing complexity and sophistication of the brain from age five to age twenty. This development is a key factor in an individual's ability to make mature judgment decisions.

THE CONNECTION CONNECTION

One fundamental of healthy sexuality is the capacity to emotionally "connect" to another person. Parents are modeling "connecting" for their children from the time they are born. Children whose parents model healthy "connecting" are fortunate indeed because their brain wiring may be healthier.

A critical human trait, one that has enormous implications for sex and relationships, is the need to connect to other human beings.[10] Parents can help a child develop this capacity.

The human brain is formed so that at birth it demands "connecting" to other human beings. Allan N. Schore of the UCLA School of Medicine puts it this way: "We are born to form attachments . . . our brains are physically wired to develop in tandem with another's, through emotional communication, beginning before words are spoken."[11]

> "We kept having sex even though I knew he was seeing other people. I just needed to be with him, I needed him to hold me. We even did it in his car. It was humiliating, but I didn't know what else to do."
>
> SAMANTHA, 20

It is a scientifically validated finding that emotionally healthy humans connect to each other. It is felt in the strangest ways. Have you ever wondered why, when another person yawns, you often do too? Have you ever thought about why you feel the pain of someone you love when they are experiencing devastating problems in their lives? Have you wondered why you can almost predict what someone else is going to say before they say it? These and other thoughts, feelings, and actions are evidence of the "connectedness" that is a common, necessary, and normal aspect of human nature. Without this connectedness, we would be not only emotionally but also physically less healthy. This connectedness comes directly from the way our brains are formed and function from even before birth.

In his book, *Social*, Matthew Lieberman explains three major aspects of our social brain. First, "connection" is obtained and maintained by social pain and social rewards. What happens when an infant is separated from his mother or when a long-term marriage ends with the death of one of the partners? The loss results in social pain, which results in seeking the social reward of being with others who care for us.[12] The importance of connection was learned years ago when it was shown that if babies are given adequate nutrition and health care but are otherwise left in their cribs untouched, they usually do not thrive and can even die.[13]

Another amazing discovery about how the brain allows us to connect with others was discovered by Italian neuroscientist Giacomo Rizzolatti when he discovered a certain kind of brain cell that he called a "mirror neuron." These neurons are responsible for allowing us to feel a loved one's pain or experience hunger when we hear someone bite into an apple. This development of empathy supports the social aspect called "mindreading," which enhances our social connections and helps us avoid the pain of rejection.[14] Mindreading is not some telepathic ability to see what the other person is thinking, but rather the mental ability to put oneself in another's position and imagine what they are going through. Mirror neurons also appear to be essential to the way children learn.[15]

Third, Lieberman describes the social realm of "harmonizing," as our brains develop self-knowledge and self-control. These disciplines help us to be more valuable to our groups, as our beliefs and values become socialized to blend with our family and friends.[16] Each of these three aspects of our social brain are associated with physical regions of our brain that have been studied with fMRI techniques. This is a vital understanding of who and what we humans are. This connectedness or social brain wiring is not only something that exists in us as human beings but is there for a purpose: it contributes to our being fully human and to our being able to accomplish those things we are capable of and want to succeed at—not just physically but also emotionally, psychologically, relationally, and so on. And as we shall see, it is necessary for building healthy, meaningful relationships that are vital for a truly fulfilled life.[17]

Well, what about sex and this concept? It may sound blunt, but if we try to eliminate this connectedness from sex, we remove the uniquely human aspect of sex and the sexual act becomes nothing more than raw animal behavior. However, when this connectedness is allowed to mature in the context of a life-long committed relationship, sex is a wonderful, sustaining expression of love and humanness.

Obviously, individuals do not carry the connectedness they have in infancy directly into adulthood, knowing exactly which person to connect with in a life-long, mutually faithful monogamous relationship. There are some interim steps, as even a cursory observation will note. So, there are stages of emotional development leading to that point:

> **"She wanted to do it. I didn't push her or anything. But when it was over she cried and acted like it was a big mistake. I wish it hadn't happened. But we can't take it back and now everything is messed up."**
>
> **ANDY, 15**

- *Infatuation or nascent love*: this is the emergence of interest in the opposite sex during adolescence. An adolescent may have very emotional and strongly felt "love" for one individual and a few months later, a similar strong feeling for another person.[18]

At this point, several divergent paths emerge. This is a critical juncture, where most people choose to engage in one of the following patterns of behavior:

- *Short-term sexual relationships*: these are sexual relationships that have very little connectedness and, according to extensive research, the least satisfying sex. The normal connecting and bonding seem not to develop in such relationships. Likely, the brain has been molded to accept this short-term pattern of relationship as normal, which can lead to a pattern of serial sex that can last for years.[19]
- *Long-term monogamy (outside of marriage):* a sexual relationship that usually results in weaker connectedness, less permanent relationships, sex with somewhat less satisfaction, and looser or no bonding. As a matter of fact, Regnerus and Uecker show the unfairness of this lifestyle for women when their research reinforces the conclusion that a sustained pattern of serial monogamy—implying a series of failed relationships—hurts women far more than it hurts men. But our emphasis here is that these monogamous sexual relationships are often not free of problems.[20]
- *Marriage:* this is the sexual relationship in which the brain is molded to facilitate healthy, rewarding, long-term connectedness. Marriage is the relationship that provides the greatest chance for satisfaction, bonding, and healthy sexual addiction.[21]

LOVE OR INFATUATION?

What can we possibly learn from neuroscience about something so indefinable and personal as love? As it turns out, we can learn a lot. What we learn can help us understand our own feelings and can also help us give guidance to our young people as they deal with the powerful emotion they often call love. But is it really?

We briefly introduced the word *infatuation* above. Let us explain it more. This emotion refers to the incredibly exciting awakening of sexual awareness embodied in focus on a person of the opposite sex. However, infatuation does not befall just preteens and young teens. It can "hit" anyone of any age. We call infatuation the great imitator of true love because it appears that the same brain centers that signal "passionate new love" to an individual are the ones that cause a more immature feeling, that of "infatuation." Therefore, it is impossible from brain study techniques as well as by social study techniques to say whether the feelings one has for another person constitute infatuation or legitimate early love.[22]

Since not even a study of the brain can tell the difference between true love and infatuation, parents as well as young people themselves should be cautious when an adolescent pronounces himself "in love." This feeling of love can be very intense, similar to obsessive-compulsive disorder, causing people to think of doing things they would not ordinarily do.[23] This intense emotional state may last several months. (There is no specific cutoff time found by scientists.) This cutoff is not sudden and may in part be due to a gradual decline in the level of dopamine because with time the romantic emotions are less intense.[24]

> "I feel like I can't trust anyone anymore. I thought he cared for me, but now I wonder if it was just all about sex for him. I don't really know how to know the difference."
>
> CHANDRA, 16

Many couples break up during this time for any number of reasons, such as other priorities (education or job), lack of common interests, personality problems, disagreements over goals, religion, and so on. Some of the reasons people break up are difficult to define. They might be included under the term *intuition*. Helen Fisher talks about us each having a "love map", which is a list of traits that we are looking for in a partner that may be subconscious.[25] One or the other or both "just know" the relationship, as intense and exciting as it is, is not right in the long run.

Having this information at hand, it is easy to see the advantages of patiently letting a relationship mature before committing to it through sexual involvement. Letting a relationship mature means taking time. Even though brain scans cannot tell whether initial infatuation will become true love, they can show the difference between the early passionate stage of romantic love and that of long-term, comfortable, and relaxed loving attachment.[26]

One very significant but sad outcome of becoming involved in an intense romantic relationship that breaks up, especially if it has become sexual, is emotional upheaval. Men can experience these feelings, but studies clearly show that women suffer more, even women older than eighteen. Regnerus and Uecker state, "Their negative emotions vary widely but can include guilt, regret, temporary self-loathing, rumination, diminished self-esteem, a sense of having used someone else or been used, a sense of having let yourself down, discomfort about having to lie or conceal sex from family, anxiety over the depth and course of the relationship, and concern over the place or role of sex in the relationship."[27]

Another reason it is best not to become involved sexually before marriage, especially if one is a teenager, is that a relationship that becomes intense and/or sexual prior to the age of twenty-one will probably not be permanent. As any adult can attest, infatuation is usually short-lived, lasting only weeks or months and not years as does true love. Statistics show that if young people begin having sex when they are sixteen years old, more than 44 percent of them will have had five or more sexual partners by the time they are in their twenties. If they are older than twenty when they initiate sex, only 15 percent will have had more than five sexual partners, while just over 50 percent will have committed sexually to only one partner.[28]

If people of any age become sexually involved before marriage, the intensity of the desire for repetition of sexual activity can overwhelm everything else in the relationship. Sex at this immature stage can keep a person from honestly evaluating the other person. Sex can make a person feel that the other person is the "right one" because the bonding and dopamine high it brings can blind one to honestly looking at the other's faults and lack of compatibility.[29] And now the warning that we will repeat throughout this book: multiple studies show that those who have sex before they marry are more likely to divorce after they do marry.[30]

HOOKED ON LOVE

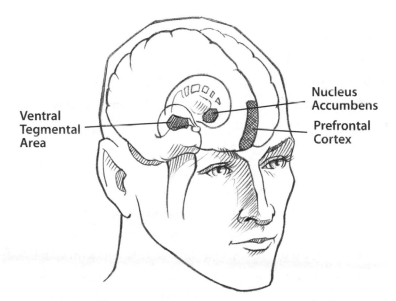

Side view of brain areas most commonly involved in mature love. Brain areas most commonly involved in mature or long-lasting and committed love.

We have seen how experience produces brain molding, both for healthy and unhealthy behaviors or experiences. This process is also powerfully at work in sustained romantic relationships. As these intense and exciting relationships develop, they cause connections between brain cells to grow stronger and more numerous. As we know, when those connections grow and cause more pleasurable behavioral experiences, more dopamine is released. This abundant outpouring of dopamine is similar to what happens in other more commonly recognized forms of addiction such as substance abuse. "Drugs such as cocaine and amphetamine target dopamine neurons."[31]

> **"We're proud of it. We set a goal to be pure for each other on our wedding day and we did it. It wasn't easy, but it taught us a lot about each other. I'm glad we did it."**
>
> DAVID, 30

In other words, love, on a biochemical level, is a lot like addiction. The healthy addiction of a lifelong monogamous sexual relationship even has measurable physical benefits. Consider what these researchers found:

Janice K. Kiecolt-Glaser and her colleagues at the Ohio State University Medical Center conducted a series of studies examining the connections between close sexual relationships, especially those of married couples, and physiological processes such as immune, endocrine, and cardiovascular functioning. These researchers report growing evidence linking relationship intimacy to better health, including stronger immune systems and physical wounds taking less time to heal. Conversely, high-conflict (anti-intimate) marital relationships appear to weaken the immune system and increase vulnerability to disease, especially among women, including worsening the body's response to proven vaccines and lengthening the amount of time required for physical wounds to heal.[32]

This is just a small example of how connectedness with a spouse is found to be associated with better health. Other research has revealed numerous benefits of individuals maintaining long-term connectedness to their mate. Harvard University began a study in 1938 called the Harvard Study of Adult Development. Nineteen of the original men participants are still living. The study has continued using descendants of the original participants and others, and is ongoing with many spin-off studies. One such study published in June 2010 concludes, "This study provides support for the role of marital satisfaction in protecting older adults' happiness from daily fluctuations in perceived physical health, and for the influence of social connections in promoting happiness in the lives of older adults."[33]

In short, brain researchers and other scientists are now clearly mapping out what might be called the biochemistry of connection.

THE SEX CONNECTION

It is probably obvious by now what the natural and healthy inclination for connectedness has to do with sex. "When biologist Justin Garcia and anthropologist Chris Reiber asked college students why they had had a recent hookup, 51% said they had hoped it would initiate a traditional romantic relationship."[34] Regnerus and Uecker discuss a number of studies that reveal this same type of information. For example, they show that girls often do not communicate their true desires and expectations about having a sexual relationship.[35] Many of them want relationship and security. As a matter of fact, they say that they "give" sex for security.[36] Women will even do things they did not want to do with a man out of concern for the fragile security of the relationship.[37] And finally, what many women want out of a sexual relationship is to settle into a stable relationship.[38] For example, 50 percent of cohabiting women (and 40 percent of cohabiting men) actually want to marry "now."[39]

One of the most startling findings of all in this brain research about love and lust is that they are each handled distinctly differently by the brain. Recent studies show certain brain centers to light up in subjects as a result of being shown pictures of their beloved. These patterns of brain activity were distinctly different from the brain activity associated with lust as shown by other experiments.[40]

This means, of course, that a man or woman can be sexually attracted to another person, approach that person for sex, engage in sex, and yet have no sincerely love-motivated thought or interest at all because all their desire arises from the brain's center for "lust." Young men and women especially need to be aware of and alert to their own feelings and to those of a potential partner. A person might approach another with a show of warmth and consideration, acts of kindness, even with words of love and commitment. But all this can be based on lust—a counterfeit emotion designed to manipulate the other into having sex, with no romantic or love interest at all.

While it is normal and not wrong for a human being to have lustful sexual urges—and lust in the context of a loving married relationship is certainly normal—it is the acting on lustful urges alone that is out of sync with human nature. This is critical to understand if we are to be emotionally healthy, and an understanding that is necessary for a future that is as free of problems as possible. Healthy human behavior demands the integration of all of what we are—body, mind, emotions, and spirit.[41] Sex practiced inappropriately can both control and damage the relationship. Not only is the relationship damaged, but the two people involved can also be.

We have already mentioned the negative consequences that young people experience in these short-term sexual relationships. It affects their brains, molding them so that short-term sexual relationships become the normal "habit" and causes them to become desensitized to the risk of short-term relationships, eventually believing that this behavior is harmless and acceptable, and does not involve the psychological and mental health part of themselves.[42] Then when they do experience the emotional and psychological problems we enumerated above from these relationships, they often are blindsided and don't even know where such feelings come from. Yet they have been told over and again that they can have sex anytime with anyone with no consequences.

In contrast, the relationship that continues long-term results in brain molding that, in a sense, helps hold the two people together for life. This brain molding, as we have examined, is due in part to the oxytocin and vasopressin secreted into the woman's and man's brains as a result of their contact with each other, initiating the cascade of change in the brain that ultimately leads to rewiring (molding) the brain and solidifying the marriage relationship. This is the deep, abiding love of a mature relationship.[43] One long-term result of the mature love relationship that stays intact (and there are many such positive results, such as providing a stable home environment for child security) is a relaxed, trusting, loving, rewarding, faithful, sexual relationship.[44]

The healthy progression of relationship strengthens the brain cell connections associated with "attachment" of one person to another, helping to ensure the permanence of the relationship that finds its healthiest expression with sexual consummation in marriage.[45]

But this natural process can be short-circuited. As we discussed earlier, during the intense early romantic period, a couple wants to be together. This togetherness can obviously include physical closeness. The physical closeness can produce sexual interest. If individuals in this early phase of their relationship spend time with intimate skin-to-skin closeness and then become sexually involved, the oxytocin and vasopressin will induce bonding and brain wiring.[46] Since this bonding has taken place before consideration of issues that could be divisive has occurred, the couple may break up when these very practical considerations intrude, as they always will. Then the breaking of the bond happens, with pain sometimes felt like physical pain, with regrets often occurring.[47] Indeed, Regnerus and Uecker have shown that the pain of a cohabiting relationship is like that of divorce.[48] Brain scans can actually "see" the changes in the brain signaling a feeling similar to physical pain when these relationships break up.

As we've discussed, oxytocin is released in the female as the behavior persists, beginning the process of bonding her to her sexual partner and creating a greater desire to repeat the activity with him. When a male engages in sex, vasopressin is released, beginning the process, as with oxytocin in the female, of bonding to his partner and also stimulating the desire for more sex. Most important, the synapses that govern decisions about sex in both the male and female brains are then strengthened in ways that make it easier to choose to have sex in the future, while synapses that govern sexual restraint are weakened and deteriorate. In short, engaging in sex creates a chain reaction of brain activities that lead to the desire for more sex and greater levels of attachment between two people.

The bonding process can also be short-circuited by a couple

progressing immediately to sex. People involved in this behavior either don't think about the risk or believe they can disconnect their sexual involvement from the rest of who they are. We have shown that this is impossible. Thus, unconscious change can occur that can motivate one to sexual behavior that can be detrimental, because it violates the integrity of personhood and because sexual interest and behavior involves the whole person, even if we don't realize it.[49]

Finally, the finding that the brain centers that produce feelings of romance and love are different and separate from the brain centers responsible for lust is a huge warning to adolescents and young adults. A selfish and manipulative person may have an intense desire to have sex with another person. To accomplish that goal, they may lie about being in love. It is important to know the desire someone has for sex can exist without any feelings of caring, love, or romance.[50] This is something that takes some life experience to recognize, which is why even young adults need to seek out guidance and advice. Research has shown that relationships started on such shallow emotional depth usually eventually break apart far more often than they succeed.[51] Individuals who go through these painful breakups, in spite of the pain, will often proceed to another sexual relationship. The science we discuss here would suggest that the release of dopamine is so exhilarating and the feeling of oxytocin and vasopressin release is so pleasurable that it draws people to subsequent sexual encounters in spite of past hurt. This is to say that with repeated sexual contact, dopamine, oxytocin, vasopressin, etc. once again are secreted into the body.

Further, there is evidence that when this sex/bonding/breaking-up cycle is repeated a few or many times—even when the bonding was short-lived—brain wiring can have occurred that causes a person to have more problems later on in developing significant and meaningful connection to other human beings because of the brain molding that can then unconsciously guide their behavior.

An obvious question is that if skin-to-skin or sexual contact causes such bonding, why don't more of these young couples stay together? And the truth is that a few do. Of course we all know examples of very young couples who become pregnant, get married, and stay married for many years. We also know teenagers who become attached to each other and the relationship drags on for months or even years in spite of one person abusing, cheating on, or degrading the other.

But for the vast majority, these relationships begun while the couple is young and unmarried are short-lived.[52] These breakups are due to any number of reasons, including attraction to another person, boredom with the current partner, a family move, opinions of peers, the distraction of other activities, even parental disapproval, among countless others. But in spite of the brevity of these sexual encounters, research indicates that some bonding and then brain molding does occur, even when a couple has only engaged in sex a single time.[53] This of course may explain why so much of the pain and regret we discussed earlier, especially for women, occurs when these breakups happen.

The point here is that if young people are not guided by parents, mentors, and other caring adults, but make their own decisions based on these less-than-optimal types of connecting, they often make poor decisions.[54] As we explained in chapter 2, this information has many implications. One implication is that, as we have shown, young people can develop early connectedness to someone they find attractive. If they feel that "this is the one for them," they can enter into progressive physical contact with that person until they have had sexual intercourse and are then even more closely bonded to the person and "addicted" to having sex with them, all as a result of unhealthy brain molding.[55]

It is important to remind all reading this that though such unhealthy bonding can result in unhealthy brain molding, it is not necessarily irreversible. A person can later on enter into marriage and have a happy and healthy marriage. The brain is moldable until death. But a person who has experienced unhealthy molding may have to have counseling or spiritual renewal or some other intervention to rewire their brain and to erase some unhealthy "creases" in their brain. Since we know that people who have had sex before they entered into marriage have a higher divorce rate than those who had not had prior sex, it may mean that even a person intent on rewiring their brain in order to enjoy a long marriage may have to endure a divorce as they get their brain "straightened out." But it is vital that we add a positive note. Lots of people who have had sex before marriage do have healthy marriages. Many have undergone counseling. Many commit themselves to working on their marriage no matter what. Our encouragement is to be observant of one's marriage and if cracks begin, then immediately do something about it. Get counseling, go to a trusted leader who is committed to marriage—do something to heal the marriage before the "cracks" become deadly for the marriage.

In a relationship of true love and long-term commitment, sex takes its appropriate place—not at the center of the relationship, but as one of the natural outcomes of the healthy connectedness of two people. Sex will then be a catalyst to the full, healthy, long-term committed relationship it strengthens.

These are the things that define us as human. True "love" includes applying this mature thought process to another in the context of romance, attachment, optimal brain molding and bonding.

Allowing such love to develop and then to guide us will lead to healthy and good decisions about behavior. Such decisions will then expand our horizons, help eliminate baggage that might weigh us down, and send us into true, life-fulfilling love.

All this adds up to show that if adults merely provide adolescents only with facts about behavior, but don't give them guidance on how to act on this information, teens and young adults cannot make the very best decisions and often will make poor decisions. It is crucial that parents and other influential adults provide adolescents with the guidance to make the best decisions based on the facts that have been presented.

Adolescent judgment, therefore, is in gradual formation and will often only achieve true maturity when shepherded by the guidance of parents or committed and caring mentors. As children grow older, the need for adult guidance naturally decreases, and yet continued adult guidance is needed for longer than most of society has realized in past years. The need for advice and counsel extends through the college-age years and for two or three years after.

In addition, the guidance of parents and other caring adults can help structurally develop the brain of a young person, thus enabling them to make the very best decisions by the time they are fully cognitively mature. This guidance allows them to have the best chance of becoming who they are meant to be and the best chance of fulfilling their dreams. Responsible parents, and those who support them, can help adolescents and sometimes even young adults avoid risky behavior that can damage them permanently. In fact, recent surveys of high school students show that parents influence the decisions they make about sex more than even their friends do.[56] Encouraging words!

TO **THINK** ABOUT

- For how long does a person's brain remain moldable? What are some ways to positively and negatively mold the developing brain?
- What happens to the brain of a person who repeats the sex/bonding/breaking-up cycle?
- The authors tell us "it is a scientifically validated finding that emotionally healthy humans connect to each other." In what ways do humans connect with one another, scientifically speaking?

WE HUMANS have a built-in desire
for attachment. When we exercise
the choices that tie us to others,
we are at our most human.

Chapter Four

BAGGAGE CLAIM

Almost everyone has sex at some point in their lives. Whether it's in high school, on a honeymoon with their soul mate, or on a one night stand, nearly every adult (and a majority of people reading this book) has experienced sex. But, as we have seen, sex is far more complicated than just a momentary physical act of pleasure; engaging in sex almost always carries long-term psychological consequences, either life-enhancing or life-limiting. The brain chemical effect of sex has happened, in varying degrees, to everyone who has experienced sexual intercourse. Does this mean that individuals who engaged in casual sex even once are somehow "broken" and cannot be fixed? What about people who have had multiple partners or lost their virginity at an early age? What about rape victims who had no choice in the matter and are left scarred by a violent sexual experience?

While important work has been done to understand and treat

> "There are so many things I want to accomplish in life. Having a child at fifteen is not one of them."
>
> SHARON, 15

the emotional scars of rape and sexual abuse, more could be accomplished with a broader understanding of how the sex act triggers the release of brain chemicals, setting off a chain reaction with profound consequences. Rather than acknowledging that sex has an impact on a person's entire being—the mental and physical, good and also sometimes bad—many choose to ignore the evidence. However, as we have seen and shall explain more here, ignorance is not "bliss."

In the interest of tolerance, acceptance, and a modern view of what is supposedly "good and right and natural" for young people, our modern society has normalized involvement in sexual activity outside the boundaries of a lifelong relationship.[1] Shame, regret, physical repercussions, and other effects on future relationships has been minimized or attributed to other factors by those who deem that it is acceptable for adolescents to engage in sexual activity when they feel they are ready. When young people do experience unfortunate problems from sex, these very same young people are blamed for their mistakes. Such blame takes multiple forms, such as "they just didn't use their condoms consistently enough" or "they thought they were emotionally mature enough but they weren't" or "the sex they had was not appropriately consensual for both persons."[2]

THE DRIVE FOR MORE

Sexual intercourse *is* a normal behavior for human beings. Without a sex drive, the human race would become extinct. Therefore, the body naturally seeks out and engages in sex as a built-in mechanism to ensure the survival of the human race. The cascade of hormonal events and then brain molding that occur in the body and brain as a result of sexual involvement are normal events and seem to almost always happen regardless of marital status, social status, ethnic makeup, education, and so on. These brain chemical effects are built into the body and are put there for good reason. For example, as we have examined, the dopamine reward that follows sexual behavior usually causes an individual to desire sex again and again once they have experienced it. Since pregnancy occurs only about 25 percent of the time with one sex act at the time of ovulation, it takes repeated encounters to assure the greatest opportunity for pregnancy, even in women of normal fertility.[3] Because survival of the human race is dependent on this occurring, the desire for sex to ensure pregnancy is built into the human body, with dopamine and other hormones seemingly at work to assure that the man and woman keep trying.

Statistics, research, and casual observation tell us that many people are responding to these natural urges outside of the context of marriage. About 40 percent of all high school students (freshmen through seniors) have had sexual intercourse.[4] Approximately 57.3 percent of graduating high school students have had sex.[5] Nearly half of all college students report having oral sex one or more times in the past 30 days.[6] During young adulthood, many young adults are sexually active and move in and out of romantic relationships. In fact, most young adults in dating relationships, which often do include sexual involvement, do not view their relationships as permanent.[7] We have already seen that the earlier an individual initiates sexual intercourse, the more likely it is that they will have multiple sexual partners. A study published by Guttmacher Institute confirmed that the most common risk factor for STIs and unintended

> "Sex just seemed like part of the date and usually took place by the second time I went out with someone. It left me feeling empty, but I figured that's the way things were. I felt lonely and hollow inside."
>
> LANEY, 26

pregnancies was having two or more sexual partners during adolescence. Forty-two percent of these adolescents reported having multiple partners. Twenty- six percent had been younger than sixteen when they first had sex. Those adolescents with a previous nonmonogamous relationship had an increased risk for having one or more sex partners in the past year.[8]

Another study had similar findings. Among females aged fifteen to twenty-four, 54 percent experienced intercourse by eighteen. Early sexual debut before fifteen was associated with a girl having sex with a separate person even as she is sexually involved with a primary sex partner. Twenty-five percent of women in these dual sexual partnerships were less than fifteen years of age when they first had sex. The odds of this type of multiple sexual partnering were much more likely (3.7 times that of women who began sex when eighteen or older) if the girl began sex before she was fifteen. It also showed that women (up to age forty-four) involved in these dual sexual partnerships reported a median of ten lifetime partners when questioned later on in the study.[9] The reason for pointing out this information is to show how people (men and women alike) involved in early sexual activity develop sexual patterns that are truly destructive to them. It seems that the dopamine reward signal, the effect of other neurochemicals, and the brain wiring are working very well in these young people. Once they experience sex, they seem to repeat it again and again. We have discussed elsewhere how sex is similar to drug, alcohol, or nicotine addiction; it is understandable that a young (or older) person would want to experience that same rush again.[10] But clearly, there are psychological and emotional factors at work in those who are very young at sexual initiation. That discussion may be outside the realm of this book, but studies do show that those who are initiated into sexual behavior at these very young ages have a high probability of becoming quite promiscuous. All this information does point out the wisdom of protecting especially our very young girls and boys from sexual involvement.

It is helpful to note that when individuals in a relationship break up and they then enter another relationship, they will tend to move quickly and prematurely to the same degree of intimacy in the new relationship that they experienced in the old one, even with partners with dissimilar intimacy patterns. In other words, if a couple has been having intercourse as a part of their relationship and then break up, each, on entering a relationship with another person, will tend to move quickly to sexual intercourse with the new partner, even if the new partner has not had sexual intercourse before.[11] The dopamine reward and the brain wiring for sex is strong.

THE PAIN OF BROKEN BONDS

As we have emphasized throughout this book, almost every time a person has sexual intercourse or intimate physical contact, bonding begins to take place.[12] Whenever breakups occur in these relationships, a person can experience depression, confusion, and often pain. Such pain can be shown in brain studies of those who have been sexually involved. This apparently happens because the brain connectedness sealed by sex has been broken.[13]

> "To be honest, I just want to get it over with. I'm scared about how it will feel and what it means. But I love him and I'm afraid he will leave me if we don't take the next step."
>
> KEISHA, 15

We see the explanation for this when we learn that when two people join physically, powerful neurohormones are released because of the sexual experience, making an impression on the synapses in their brains and hardwiring their bond, essentially molding their brains to connect to each other. When they stay together for life, their brains have developed a strong connection between the two. Apparently, this is a major factor that keeps a married couple together, providing desire for intercourse, resulting in offspring, and assuring those offspring of a nurturing two-parent home in which to grow.[14]

The longer people are together, the stronger their connection can become. When that connection is broken, more problems can result than simply the loss of the relationship. The neurochemical imprint of that sexual experience remains, often for many years, and can make the bonding and then brain molding for a future healthy relationship more difficult. This pattern can damage one of the most important abilities humans are born with: the ability to connect at a deep and abiding level to another person.[15] The brain molding that enables healthy long-term relationships resides in some of the deepest and most fundamental parts of the human brain, and when damaged may require years of counseling for even the most committed person to heal.

On its most basic level, it seems that young people feel that something very important to themselves has been damaged by these sexual relationships that are so temporary. Perhaps they feel that their ability to connect or bond to others is in danger. Because the ability to connect is so vital to our being emotionally healthy functioning human beings, these young people intuitively sense that something is desperately wrong, though they may have trouble articulating what it is. These disturbed impressions may lead to depression and even suicidal thoughts.

We should not be surprised at these stark statements. In chapter 1, we looked at some of the statistics that demonstrate these impressions, but the information bears repeating here. A study that measured adolescent depression and sexual experience shows that about 45 percent of depressed adolescents had engaged in sexual intercourse. The youngest age groups for both boys and girls who were depressed were more likely than their peers to have experienced sexual intercourse. More fourteen- to sixteen-year-olds experienced such depression than older teens. Younger depressed boys were almost five times more likely to have experienced sex than those who were not depressed. Additionally, data from the 2017 Youth Risk Behavioral Surveillance (YRBS) reported sexually active students attempted suicide more than those who had no sexual contact.[16]

The spring 2017 *American College Health Association Survey* reported that 32.7 percent of male students and 41.3 percent of female students felt so depressed during the previous year that it was sometimes hard for them to function. Almost as telling was the finding that 43.7 percent of male students and 53.9 percent of female students felt that "things were hopeless" at some point in the past year. Also, approximately 10.3 percent of students reported seriously considering attempting suicide at least once during the previous year, and approximately 1.5 percent had actually attempted suicide in the past year.[17] This and other studies indicate that some of this psychological stress, depression, and suicide ideation is due to the sexual involvement of these young people.[18] Exactly how much is unclear according to the available data.[19] Additionally, adolescents who learn they are infected with an STD (one in four sexually active adolescents has an STD) are more likely to suffer from depression at much higher rates than those who are not affected.[20] These findings may explain why so many teens who chose to have sex during their teen years later regretted it and wished they had waited.[21]

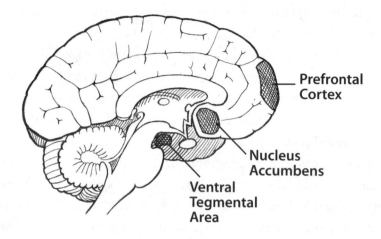

The locations of the brain believed to be most involved with depression.

Several years ago during the course of a routine exam, a thirty-five-year-old Texas woman was asked about her history of sexual activity. She specifically remembered her first experience and related how painful it was. She confided that she had never enjoyed sex and in fact had "hated every minute of it." She described negative thoughts and bad memories of sexual experiences that came back to her while in the shower or in bed. To her, sexual activity is "something that literally stays with a person for an entire lifetime."[22]

Becoming sexually active and having multiple sexual partners may sometimes damage an individual's ability to develop healthy, mature, and long-lasting relationships later on. This seems to hold true especially for a future healthy and stable marriage. Recent studies show an association between sex before marriage and marital problems in some subsequent marriages. For example, the more sexual partners a person had before marriage, the more likely he or she is to divorce than those who waited or had fewer partners before marrying.[23] This suggests, among other things, that the person's brain wiring has made a person accustomed to intermittently changing sexual partners, which is of course a problem once a person is in a marriage relationship. This can sometimes cause a person in the marriage to struggle with the commitment that comes with marriage. The example occasionally used in sexual risk avoidance classes of sticking a piece of tape on a kid's arm, pulling it off and sticking it on again, showing that it is less able to stick with each new attempt, is erroneous. This is not how this complicated sexual bonding and brain molding works. It is much more complicated than that. However, this is not to say that multiple sexual partners before marriage cannot cause problems. That pattern from the past can indeed cause problems in a marriage.

The encouraging news is that studies clearly show that this does not *always* happen. However, a couple who has had sex before marriage, particularly those who have had sex with someone other than their eventual wife or husband, should not wait very long to confront a problem in their relationship if it develops. They should take action even if it involves counseling if they begin seeing such fractures in their relationship. If they do not do this, they may be at increased risk for unhappiness in marriage or even divorce.[21]

COLLATERAL DAMAGE

Although this book is primarily about the third risk—the effects of sex on the brain—we would be remiss not to touch on the other two risks as well. STDs and unwanted pregnancies are part of the greater discussion, since they also affect people's mental and emotional states. In addition to the brain chemical effects of sex that have already been discussed, bodily fluids and secretions are exchanged between partners during sexual contact. The exchange occurs not only during intercourse, but also during other activities such as genital touching, oral sex, and anal sex (anal sex being by far the most dangerous). If a person has a sexually transmitted infection, sometimes

"We know we shouldn't really have sex, so we just do oral stuff. That way everyone stays safe from diseases and no one gets in trouble."

MICHAEL, 18

the germs of that infection are in the person's bodily fluids, sometimes they are on the skin, especially of the genital area, and sometimes both. Those germs can then infect their partner with herpes, gonorrhea, HPV, or other diseases one of them might be infected with—even without sexual intercourse, since some of these germs can be passed from skin-to-skin contact.

Each year, a whopping 20 million new cases of sexually transmitted disease are contracted in the United States. Half of these are in people under the age of twenty-five.[25] In 2016, there were more than 2 million new cases of the three reportable STDs reported in the United States. These included chlamydia, gonorrhea, and syphilis.[26] While much work remains to be done in educating the public about sexually transmitted infections, it is obvious that the physical dangers of sex with multiple partners such as STDs and nonmarital pregnancy are far more widely acknowledged than the psychological and emotional dangers this book speaks of.[27] Therefore, the debate over safer sex, condom use, sex education in schools, and national health policy are best left for another venue. The purpose of this book is to relay new neuroscientific research suggesting that sex involves the *entire* person, physically, mentally, emotionally—essentially all of who they are. The physical ramifications of nonmarital sex should not be ignored, but neither should the emotional effects. A common error is to believe that the emotional impact is just a feeling and is not that significant. This concept, as we have now shown, is not only wrong but dangerously misleading; these emotions and feelings arise from the way one's brain is molded.

For example, consider the young woman at a clinic in Mississippi who was informed that she had herpes, a sexually transmitted infection that causes outbreaks of painful blisters in the genital area. There is no cure for the condition but only a regimen of treatment that works to prevent or minimize future outbreaks. Shocked and dismayed, the young patient reacted with tears and angry denial. After the initial surprise had subsided, her doctor began to discuss transmission—how she acquired it, from whom, and when. Eventually, the conversation turned to the possibility of her having sex in the future. "If I did," she said, "I would not be able to tell anyone that I had herpes." Her shame and regret was so great, she claimed she would be willing to endanger another person rather than face the consequences of an open and honest disclosure of her infection. Sadly, this scenario plays out in the lives of people across the country every day.[28]

Similarly, out-of-wedlock pregnancy has a dramatic impact on the course of life for the mother, the father, and the unborn child. Unmarried teen mothers are more likely to drop out of school, receive welfare, have mental and physical health problems, continue to have out-of-wedlock pregnancies, and, even if they subsequently marry, are more likely to divorce.[29] For example, less than two-thirds of teen mothers graduate from high school or earn a GED within two years of giving birth.[30] Here are more specifics:

- Among teen fathers, 46 percent were neither married nor cohabiting with the mother by ages 22 to 24[31]
- 63 percent of teen mothers receive public assistance within the first year of a child's birth[32]

- 52 percent of mothers on welfare had their first child in their teens[33]
- On average, custodial single parents who receive child support get about $329 per month to cover all child needs[34]
- Nearly 30 percent of single parents do not receive any due child support money[35]

These startling statistics are no secret. That's why enormous efforts have been made to encourage contraceptive use by sexually active teenagers. A health-care provider may consider this appropriate, but, as the science of this book shows, other significant problems beside unplanned pregnancy can result from nonmarital sex. Consequently, we would suggest that providers entertain contraception as an option only if they provide intense, one-on-one counseling, rather than giving an open-ended prescription. For contraception—if the health-care provider is going to prescribe such—we suggest the prescriber should, particularly for the adolescent, see such a prescription only as a stopgap until the adolescent returns to abstinence—a change in behavior much more common than conventional wisdom would indicate.[36] However, when considering the statistics gathered during all these years of emphasis on contraceptive use, we suggest that young people and older single individuals be taught to consider their entire sexual behavior pattern and not just how to avoid an unplanned pregnancy. That said, the likelihood of a pregnancy even with the strong contraceptive emphasis that most young people (and this includes individuals in their young 20s, also) have been exposed to is higher than most realize. To ignore the facts that have now been gathered during years of contraceptive/condom emphasis is to put one's head in the sand

and leave other young people at significant risk of nonmarital pregnancy. For example:

- In a 2012 report, 21 percent of teens became pregnant despite using a highly effective contraceptive method[37]
- About 20 percent of males and females using condoms get pregnant within one year[38]
- About 9 percent of adult women using oral contraceptives become pregnant in their first year of use[39]
- About one in two women used emergency contraception because they feared failure of the contraceptive method[40]
- Among women who were not trying to get pregnant, cohabiters report that about 20 percent of cohabiting women using contraception experienced a pregnancy within the first year of cohabiting[41]

Adolescent brain molding often results in young people developing a pattern of sexual activity that often leads them to continue that activity.[42] This activity will, as we see from the above data, often lead to pregnancy, regardless of contraceptive or condom use. Pregnancy can have lifelong consequences for the unmarried girl, the father (especially if he is a teenager), and the child that results. It often results in none of these three primary people involved ever achieving their hopes and dreams or achieving their potential. And, of course, condoms and contraceptives provide no protection from the influences of sex on the brain.

"I HAD NO CHOICE"

Unfortunately, not everyone chooses when or how they will experience sex. Many people have fallen victim to sexual abuse during

> **"I was so drunk the first time that I don't really remember it. But now that my virginity is gone, it doesn't make any sense not to have sex. I've already done it, so I might as well have fun."**
>
> **SUSAN, 19**

childhood or as a teenager. According to The Rape, Abuse and Incest National Network's (RAINN) research, of those who have been victims under the age of eighteen, two out of three are ages twelve to seventeen.[43] Rape and sexual coercion are the most extreme forms of unhealthy sexual behavior. They are violent acts of aggression against the victim. Unfortunately, these tragedies are very common. However, we can learn a great deal about the impact of sex on an individual when we explore this problem. Here are some stats:

- One in five women and one in seventy-one men will be raped at some point in their lives[44]
- Twenty to 25 percent of college women and 15 percent of college men are victims of forced sex during their time in college[45]
- In eight out of ten cases of rape, the victim knew the perpetrator[46]

The brain's response to sexual assault is different from its response to consensual sex. When our lives are threatened, the "thinking" portion of our brain (the frontal cortex) is taken over by the "defense circuitry." Brain circuitry merely means the brain's network of connections, and this just means that different centers of the brain are working together for a common cause. In the "defense circuitry," different parts of the brain work together to defend our very existence. When these threats occur, the brain almost always responds with habits and reflexes rather than with rational thinking.[47] For example, if a girl has used her skills of argument or excuse to ward off boys who have tried to talk her into sex in the past, then she may automatically use that "habit" to try to stop a rapist, which, of course, would be totally ineffective.

The first response of the brain when violence is initiated is to prepare the body for fight, flight, or freeze by releasing a surge of stress chemicals. We have all heard of fight or flight, but an extreme survival reflex that can often occur is for the threatened person to freeze. This is often the reaction of a rape victim. They are literally paralyzed by fear and they are simply unable to speak or cry out, much less move. The victim may also collapse, going completely limp or may "dissociate" from the attack psychologically and feel that the attack is unreal. By understanding how "thinking and memory" are shut down, we can better understand why rape victims respond the way they do and often have trouble describing their attacker, or focus on some obscure detail, rather than recall the exact attack.[48]

Following a sexual assault, oxytocin is often released after the body senses that it is "safe." We see here a different yet related function of the neurohormone oxytocin, as it helps the body recover from the stress response and return to a sense of well-being. This complicated recovery system seems to be strongly affected by the social situation, as well as by oxytocin, and more research is needed to better explain this recovery system.[49]

Post-Traumatic Stress Disorder (PTSD) can occur when recovery after a traumatic event is not complete. It happens more frequently in women than in men. The sense of fear does not fade as in a normal recovery, and the stress response may often be set off with the slightest reminder of the traumatic event. Oxytocin is currently being studied as a treatment for PTSD and has showed some promising results.[50]

Child Sexual Abuse

- One in four girls and one in six boys will be sexually abused before they turn eighteen years old[51]
- Three percent of girls were age ten or younger at the time of their first rape/victimization, and 30 percent of girls were between the ages of eleven and seventeen[52]
- The average age at which girls are recruited into prostitution is twelve to fourteen years of age, and the average age for boys is eleven to thirteen years old[53]
- Thirty-four percent of people who sexually abuse a child are family members[54]

A singular sexual assault can cause incredible damage to a person, and chronic sexual assault can be utterly devastating. When sexual abuse begins in childhood, it often is repeated in adolescence and adulthood. Almost half of victimized children experience sexual abuse in the future.[55] These children who are revictimized in adolescence are fourteen times more likely to experience rape or attempted rape in their first year of college.[56]

The symptoms displayed by children who have been sexually abused vary widely and often depend on the severity, duration, and frequency of the sexual abuse they experienced.[57] But the results of the sexual abuse can often follow the victims into adulthood. A proportion of victims carry profound psychological distress into adulthood. It is thought that the symptoms themselves—including low self-esteem, distrust, and a lack of confidence—make victims more vulnerable to revictimization.[58] There is also a clear link between child sexual abuse and high-risk sexual behaviors, such as sexual promiscuity and even prostitution.[59]

Women's most common emotional responses to previous childhood sexual abuse are depression, anxiety, and anger. However, women can also experience physical symptoms such as chronic pelvic pain, abdominal discomfort, vaginal pain, and painful urination. About 80 percent of men who have been sexually assaulted abuse alcohol and/or drugs.[60] Men who have been sexually abused are more likely to engage in risky sexual behavior and to suffer from anxiety disorders and PTSD than men who have not been abused.[61] Members of both sexes report marriage and family problems.[62]

Teen Sexual Violence

Teen Dating Violence is a subject of much concern in our middle and high schools today. Often, the violence is divided into three categories: physical, emotional, and sexual. The 2017 Youth Risk Behavior Surveillance reported that out of the 68.3 percent of students nationwide who dated, 6.9 percent had been forced to do sexual acts such as kissing, touching, or intercourse in the past year.[63]

When we look carefully at teen dating violence, we see that 42.9 percent of those reporting sexual violence experienced the same abuse from two or more partners.[64] Statistics also tell us that 22 percent of women and 15 percent of men who are adult victims of rape, physical violence, and stalking by an intimate partner, first experienced teen dating violence.[65]

> **"That's how you get a boyfriend. No one will go out with me unless they think I will go all the way. I don't want to be alone. So I have to do it."**
>
> AMANDA, 14

87

Further, having been sexually abused as a child is a risk factor for becoming a victim of sexual dating violence.[66]

While sexual abuse is not experienced by the majority of individuals, we can still learn some important lessons from the experiences of those who have faced that tragedy. Among those lessons are the following:

- The impact of sex on the brain can be long-lasting;
- The impact of sex can affect future health and behavior in ways we would never expect unless forewarned; and
- Whether sex is forced, consensual, a one-night stand, or in a healthy marriage, its impact is significant and remarkable.

Once again, we can infer that past experiences guide the development of the brain in these unfortunate situations in an unhealthy way, which can then result in future unhealthy behavior or emotional problems.

MIND GAMES

In addition to rape, unwanted sex often occurs in cases of sexual manipulation. These are instances in which individuals willfully mislead or employ deceptive tactics to trick or entice others into sex in ways that cannot legally be called rape but yet verge on rape. It is helpful to mention a newsworthy event that was reported not long ago to put this issue in perspective. This story about high school seniors manipulating young women for years probably never would have come to our attention if one guy had not stepped over the line and actually raped a girl. Even then, the story would have probably been buried if the girl had not been fifteen and underage for giving consent. The sad message for all of us is that these high school seniors, year after year, seemed to feel that society around them said this kind of near-rape was acceptable behavior and that they themselves seemed to see no problem with their actions.

The story hit the national news in *The New York Times* on August 18, 2015, about the trial of a senior student at the elite St. Paul's School in Concord, New Hampshire. St. Paul's is an Episcopal preparatory school that is extremely selective and has as alumni people such as former Secretary of State John Kerry and Cornelius Vanderbilt III.

Owen Labrie, a senior student at St. Paul's, was charged with rape but was convicted in August of 2015 on lesser charges of sexual assault and endangering the welfare of a child as well as a felony charge of computer-related seduction.[67] At the time of reporting, Labrie was free on bail but will be required to register as a sex offender for the rest of his life. But the story about Labrie, who, at the time of his trial, had already been accepted to Harvard to study theology, is almost more alarming than this one student's criminal act.

Apparently, a tradition called "Senior Salute" was established at St. Paul's in 1971, when women were first admitted to the school. The goal of the ritual is for older men to pressure younger women for as much intimacy as they can get away with. This tradition was then passed down from senior class to senior class. And it became a contest among the guys to try to beat their peers by seeing if they could "score" more than the others. According to testimony, Labrie told police that he was "trying to be No. 1 in the sexual scoring at St. Paul's School."[68] Their record was shared on a "sexual scoreboard" posted on a dorm wall and online.

Labrie thought for months about what he wanted to do. Labrie wooed his victim by email with hints of romance. She said, "Here's a person who paid special attention to me."[69] Then on May 30, 2014, Labrie took the fifteen-year-old girl to a mechanical room on campus, put on a condom and, with physical and verbal intimidation, sexually assaulted her. Shamus Khan, an alumnus and now an associate professor of sociology at Columbia University, writes in his book *Privilege: The Making of an Adolescent Elite at St. Paul's School*, "There was the common denominator of sex and sexuality as the pathway to belonging and 'welcoming' for girls."[70] As troubling as this is, the statements by Labrie's defense lawyer were much more troubling when he said to the court, "The girls would be honored and proud about this, that they were the focus of the senior salute" and that some of the young women willingly took part.[71]

The recent revelations of powerful men sexually abusing women over whom they held power has brought attention to issues such as this at St. Paul's. These recent stories have produced outrage, as they should. And perhaps occurrences such as those and the experience at St. Paul's will begin to protect women. Still, as this book pointedly reminds us, young people, especially young women, often choose to engage in sexual behavior that they assume is appropriate because society around them, such as the tradition at St. Paul's, says it is the right way to live.[72]

Just because sexual intercourse is not technically rape or forced does not mean that it is truly and fully consensual or appropriate, especially for younger boys and girls. Without proper guidance, adolescent males often misunderstand or choose to ignore anything short of a flat refusal to becoming more physical in a relationship. Perhaps a discussion with our sons should begin with what consent is *not*. RAINN has this posted on its website:

- Refusing to acknowledge "no"
- Assuming that wearing certain clothes, flirting, or kissing is an invitation for anything more

- Someone being under the legal age of consent, as defined by the state
- Someone being incapacitated because of drugs or alcohol
- Pressuring someone into sexual activity by using fear or intimidation
- Assuming you have permission to engage in a sexual act because you've done it in the past.[73]

Another warning sign for parents and mentors to watch for in young people is involvement in risky behavior such as alcohol, marijuana, or tobacco abuse. The adolescent brain is more susceptible to harm from these substances than the adult brain and more susceptible to dependency on these as well.[74] We also know that when teens engage in one risky behavior, such as drinking alcohol, they are more likely to engage in other risky behaviors, such as sex.[75]

It may be that the innate human desire for meaningful connections that all people have causes many young men and women to become involved in casual sexual behavior. Without adult guidance, their natural desire for connectedness and an equally natural interest in sex will often lead to bad decisions. The National Campaign to Prevent Teen Pregnancy (now called Power to Decide) has conducted national surveys of youth in the United States for years. They consistently find that high majorities of teens who had become sexually active wish they had waited until they were older to initiate sexual activity.[76] This same organization found in a survey that 87 percent of teenagers think that young people ought to receive a strong abstinence message.[77] This obviously includes teenagers who have had sex (since almost half of the teens in high schools across the country have had sexual intercourse).[78]

The problems young people have experienced with voluntary

sex may not be as immediate, obvious, or violent as the problems of rape or coerced sex, but they are nonetheless very real and quite prevalent.

HOPE FOR THE FUTURE

The adolescent and young adult brain is far from its final, fully formed state. Because it does not reach full cognitive maturity until the midtwenties, it lacks the circuits necessary to make the best behavior decisions, the decisions that will help the individual be as free as possible of baggage from the past that can prevent the individual from achieving his or her potential.

"It was the hardest thing we ever did, but we are so glad we waited. We had to talk through our disagreements. We couldn't just feel close by having sex; we had to really work things out."

CHARLES, 28

As we have seen, the ideal situation in which a child is raised is a home in which the child has two married, biological parents.[79] Studies are clear about this. Studies of families of married parents with adopted children are incomplete. Common sense would say that the children adopted into such homes are fortunate indeed and certainly more likely to flourish in life than if left in foster or orphan homes. And fortunately, there are many, many hardworking single parents with extended families and with mentors to help, and many remarkably successful people come from such environments.

Humans have a built-in desire for attachment. When we exercise the choices that tie us to others, we are at our most human. However, because of immaturity, poorly directed peers, the pressure of society, the attraction of sex to which they are prematurely exposed, abuse, and a myriad of other factors, young people can become involved in behavior patterns that function like bad habits. These bad habits are actually brain molding and can produce major problems for the young person in the future. These unfortunate experiences can pattern the brain to make the young person repeat destructive behavior and suffer lifelong consequences, often impairing hope of achieving their life dreams and goals, even if they were born with the gifts and potential of achieving them.

Children, adolescents, and young adults need guidance to make good decisions. This guidance needs to continue, though more indirectly, into the midtwenties. When the young person receives and wisely heeds this appropriate guidance, his or her brain is actually being molded to almost habitually make behavior decisions that will facilitate their dreams and desires.

TO THINK ABOUT

- Why does the cycle of short-term sexual activity with different partners tend to repeat itself?
- What are some consequences of inadvisable sexual activity?
- Sex is just one aspect of personhood. What are others? Why can't sex be separated from what it means to be a person?

WE HAVE A responsibility to ourselves to discover our purpose and live it out. Understanding this should encourage us, if we want to reach our fullest potential, to do things that are stretching, difficult, challenging, and may even seem unnatural.

Chapter Five

THINKING LONG-TERM

The material presented so far in this book is certainly sobering, isn't it?

We've learned that research into the makeup of our bodies and our brains suggests that it is best for us to delay sexual activity until we are in a lifelong relationship, ideally marriage. In this chapter, we'll review some of the benefits of making a lifelong commitment. We will also address the various relationship types that are becoming more prevalent among young people and emerging adults. We know that many get derailed from the best life they could have had by making decisions that cause them regret. But we'll also talk about why, if a person has made less than optimal choices in the past, that doesn't mean it's the end of the story, because our complex and amazing brain is a moldable structure.

Those who have been keeping up on this subject know that

> **"I didn't know how to be in a relationship and not have sex. That was how I kept men interested, how I kept them with me. It's why they liked me. Or at least that's what I thought."**
>
> **AMY, 25**

many people in our society today choose to have sex outside of a lifelong committed relationship. A national survey of ever-married people aged fifteen to forty-four reported that 89 percent of men and 88 percent of women had premarital sex in 2011–2015.[1] Pre-marital sex particularly occurs with young people. They do this for countless reasons, justifying and rationalizing it according to their own circumstance. *It seems that the most common reason is "Because that is just the way it is. I don't really have any other choice." Or He really cares about me . . . She said she wanted to . . . We didn't want to wait . . . I was curious about what it felt like . . . I was tired of being a virgin . . . I just wanted to get it over with,* and so on. Most believe that they had special, unique, or justifiable reasons for their decision. Many, however, just seem to "do sex" because it seems to be the expected behavior.

Despite their differences, all of these people have at least one thing in common: they cannot predict the future. No one knows for certain how a relationship will work out, and a lot of people, guys especially, don't want to consider it a relationship at all. While it's *possible* that a couple having sex outside of marriage will one day make a lifelong commitment to each other, it is more likely they won't. Repetitive sexual relationships and experiences don't usually lead to better marital odds. They just lead to more sex.[2]

Today's emerging adults (those eighteen and older, even up to the late twenties) are often delaying marriage and are also increasingly open to or just "falling into" alternative relationship arrangements.

This is not to say that anyone is condemned to a second-rate life if they've had sex outside of marriage or if they have entered another sexual arrangement other than marriage. However, research clearly indicates that doing so can mean taking serious chances with one's future health and happiness. And as we have seen, it means risking much more than a sexually transmitted disease or pregnancy. We now know that there is a further risk—the danger of molding one's mind in a way that makes it more difficult in the future to experience the joys of a lifetime loving relationship.[3] Our goal in this book is to provide data to readers that show there are more risks with some choices than with others.

Life is difficult enough without the added challenges we've discussed. An individual who is forewarned about the consequences of a decision or behavior and acts to avoid that behavior will likely experience a better life, now and in the future. This information is not offered as a moral statement. Rather, the information is based on the data that supports the fact that sexual activity outside of marriage poses risks other than STDs and nonmarital pregnancy—such as emotional, psychological, and relational problems—and that sex within the context of a marriage is the ideal behavior for minimizing such problems. Still, this does not mean that individuals who disregard it or who unintentionally experience a sexual situation are destined to a life of failure and unhappiness. Clearly, even an individual who makes the best choices can be a victim of rape, molestation, or other situations, or face sexually related problems even in their own marriage. In addition, now that we have shown that the brain is moldable into old age, we can reassure those who seem to habitually make unwise sexual behavior choices that they can (with commitment, counseling, spiritual resources, and time) rewire their brains to enable them to begin habitually making good decisions with little risk and more positive outcomes, such as a healthy marriage with low probability of divorce. The likelihood of people leading fulfilled lives with less baggage to carry greatly increases by practicing sex within the healthiest context.

CASUAL SEX

The riskiest sexual situations involve an increasing number of sexual partners, with minimal or no commitment. This arrangement is commonly called "hooking up." Surveys of college students indicate hooking up can mean anything from kissing to oral sex to penetrative intercourse. A similar arrangement, referred to as "friends with benefits," involves a couple that has sex without any obligation, promise, or plans to develop a relationship—and without any (intended) emotional attachment.

Patterns of uncommitted sexual activity defy an easy label, although what is certain is that such behavior is rampant among American youth. The following statistics are sobering and underscore the number of teens and young adults who engage in sexual activity, which includes oral and anal sex:

High School Students

- Nationwide, about 40 percent of high school students have had sexual intercourse[4]
- About half of adolescents aged fifteen to nineteen reported having oral sex[5]
- One in ten adolescents reported having anal sex with an opposite partner[6]
- 57.3 percent of graduating high school seniors have had sexual intercourse[7]
- Nationwide, about 10 percent of high school students have had four or more sexual partners during their life[8]

College Students

- 41.2 percent of males and 43.9 percent of females have had sex with at least one partner in the past year[9]

- 43.9 percent of males and 49.8 percent of females reported having vaginal sex in the past thirty days[10]
- 45.1 percent of males and 44.9 percent of females reported having oral sex in the past thirty days[11]

These statistics corroborate much of what has already been mentioned. The younger teenagers are when they first engage in sexual activity, the more sexual partners they will likely have had by the time they are interviewed again in their twenties.[12] Sexual behavior for the younger teenagers, once it has commenced, appears almost compulsive. This correlates with neuroscientific findings that sex has an addictive effect on the brain and also wires the brain to accept multiple sexual partnering as "normal." Science clearly demonstrates that not everyone who has sex will experience these problems. However, a person cannot foresee whether or not they will be negatively affected. Avoiding risky behavior certainly lessens the probability.

ROMANTIC SEXUAL RELATIONSHIPS

What about romantic relationships that become sexual? By the time a dating couple reaches their senior year in high school, the majority of them have become sexually active.[13] Teens that are still living at home are usually not cohabiting. So what we know about these adolescent romances is that they are not comparable to adult romantic relationships.[14] They tend to be brief in duration and very emotionally intense.[15] So because these sexual relationships that young people become involved in are often short-lived and because they will often become involved sexually in subsequent romantic relationships, they often experience an increasing number of partners over a lifetime.[16]

LIVING TOGETHER: JUST ANOTHER CHOICE?

Are there solid, proven reasons not to move in together and live as though married? Yes.

The number of cohabiting relationships reached about 18 million in 2016.[17] It's clear that people choose to live with a significant other without the added commitment of marriage. Couples sometimes see this as a trial phase, a time to learn about each other and find out if they are compatible. Some couples may be monogamous and very much in love, but research indicates that this is a dangerous choice for their futures. Those who study this arrangement, also known as cohabitation, find that a large group of individuals enter that relationship with no plans for the relationship to lead to marriage. They simply enjoy the comfort and convenience of living and having sex with a partner and are satisfied until something happens to make them unhappy and then they move on. Sometimes they enter this arrangement because they are in love. In their book *Premarital Sex in America*, Regnerus and Uecker share a quote from a young woman that sums up this casual mindset: "I think if you're romantically involved with someone and you know them and can trust them pretty well, it's not a big deal to live with them, I guess— it's what people do."[18]

Cohabitation has become common. Between 50–70 percent of couples today are thought to be cohabiting before marrying.[19] In fact, approximately the same number of young people (by the age of twenty) live in cohabiting relationships as are married (20 percent).[20] People in a cohabiting relationship may eventually find that they want to be married. Just under half of cohabiting young women and 40 percent of cohabiting men say they'd like to be married right now.[21] But, more often, they do not decide to marry, as studies show that only one in five cohabiting relationships progress to marriage.[22]

Cohabitation is a compromise—a partial commitment in exchange for the rights and benefits that research shows are enjoyed most within a lifelong commitment. Evidence also shows that an intimate relationship with an "out clause" generally does not fulfill the anticipation of those who choose such an arrangement. Rather than providing benefits of commitment, this type of relationship often produces problems.

Consider the following facts:

- Cohabiting relationships are not equivalent to marital relationships. "Couples who perceive cohabitation as a substitute for marriage are least likely to be married five years later."[23]
- Cohabiting couples experience premarital childbearing. "Nearly twenty percent of women experienced a pregnancy in the first year of their first premarital cohabitation."[24]
- Those that cohabit before marrying are more likely to divorce[25] or separate. "For both men and women, cohabitation doubles the likelihood of thinking and talking about separating, as well as actually doing so."[26]
- Cohabiting couples experience violent behavior much more often than married couples. "Aggression is at least twice as common in cohabiting households as it is among married-parent families."[27]

The reason for pointing out these issues of cohabitation is not to criticize people who have chosen this lifestyle (though these facts should forewarn individuals considering cohabitation or who are presently in such a relationship) but to indicate how the neurochemicals and the brain centers associated with love and sex seem to work and why the bonding and subsequent brain molding that is so powerful in marriage seems less so in cohabiting relationships.

Research suggests that essentially every romantic physical contact between two people results in some degree of bonding.[28] However, such bonding requires reinforcement, the best of which appears to be in marriage. We know from studies that cohabiting couples report lower relationship quality than married couples do.[29] For example, cohabiters report more conflict, more violence, and lower levels of satisfaction and commitment.[30] Married husbands and fathers are significantly more involved and affectionate with their wives and children than are men in cohabiting relationships (with or without children).[31] The finding that cohabiting couples report lower relationship quality may explain why studies show that, in general, the absence of a binding agreement, which perhaps signals an uncertain future, reduces commitment, trust, and emotional investment when compared to marriage.[32]

In fact, cohabitation is characterized by the uncertain nature, limits, and future of the relationship.[33] These limitations are usually defined at the outset of the relationship and agreed upon by both parties. One limitation common to cohabiting relationships is that there is no long-term commitment of moving in together as a step toward marriage.[34] This can often limit the potential for the couple to become truly intimate and have a long-lasting relationship. Not making sound relationship decisions can lead to decreased relationship quality and commitment as well as to infidelity.[35]

Infidelity is still widely viewed as destructive to relationships, and most people, regardless of relationship status, expect sexual exclusivity from their partner.[36] Studies show, however, that infidelity is common in any sexual relationship arrangement outside of a healthy marriage. Regnerus, in his book *Cheap Sex*, quotes a woman who has had multiple sex partners and who had cheated on one of her sex partners several times saying, "I'd be heartbroken if someone was cheating on me."[37]

In cohabiting relationships, a factor that has been studied is the concept of "sliding into relationships" where things go unplanned or just happen without the couple making clear decisions.[38] Today, it is common for cohabitating couples to have initiated their relationship by sliding into cohabitation without thoughtfully mapping out how the transition might affect their relationship for the present, let alone the future. Low-level commitment prior to beginning their cohabitation arrangement can cause conflicts down the road if the relationship continues. For example, the longer a cohabiting relationship continues, the less likely it is that the outcome will be marriage.[39] This is in spite of the fact that after they become a cohabiter, 55 percent of cohabiting women and 40 percent of cohabiting men prefer to be married "now."[40]

> **"What is love? I don't think I ever really knew, although I thought I did. Now I wonder if I have ever really loved or been loved. It all got so tangled with sex. I think it is going to take me a long time to get it all sorted out."**
>
> **TIM, 25**

Another reason for cohabiting relationships ending sooner than marriages may be that the couple knew each other for such a short time before initiating sexual intercourse and cohabitation. A National Center for Biotechnology Information (NCBI) study revealed that among initial cohabiters, over a quarter became sexually involved within the first week of the relationship, and one-third moved in together within six months of starting the relationship.[41] The quickest transition to sexual involvement occurred among those currently cohabiting.[42] The more immediate the sexual consummation of a relationship, the more it may lead to errors in judgment about the other person. In contrast, those in the study who had married directly, without living together first, had deferred sexual intimacy for over six months.[43] This time of sexual restraint seems to allow a couple time to get to know each other without the "distraction" of "having sex." Note that although bonding in both instances can take place, as a prior chapter explained, a woman can begin to trust a man because of oxytocin secretion and, thus, ignore the warning signs of an unwise relationship decision especially if that relationship becomes sexual too soon.

Many people in our society are not convinced that marriage fosters the benefits that research suggests:

- Marriage is a clear, mutual, unambiguous signal of commitment.[44]
- Marriage results in increased family stability. It is also shown to increase the educational attainment of the married couple and also of their children. Marriage also reduces likelihood of poverty.[45]
- Marriage is also the optimal setting for childrearing[46] as shown by multiple studies comparing the outcomes of children raised in single parent homes vs. homes with two parents present.
- Marriage also tends to be good for emotional intimacy as well as sexual intimacy.[47] Individuals who have sex within the context of marriage can have greater assurance of the relationship lasting than those who are in a monogamous relationship but unmarried. Regnerus and Uecker state that few nonmarital sexual relationships survive.[48]

Most young adults hope to one day fall in love, commit, and marry.[49] And despite the societal messages we may be receiving to the contrary, 93–96 percent of both men and women plan to get married.[50] Ultimately, a healthy marriage reaps the benefits of happiness, stability, higher education, and wealth,[51] as well as satisfaction in emotional and sexual intimacy.[52] Cohabiting relationships, by definition, lack the key ingredient of long-term commitment that helps seal neurochemical and brain-molded bonds that help sustain two individuals for a lifetime.

SEX: ANY TIME, ANY PLACE, ANY . . . BODY?

Consider these questions:

Why shouldn't we have sex whenever we want to with whomever we want to?

Since animals have, as do humans, all these brain hormones and sex hormones circulating, why don't animals experience love as humans do?

Why do dogs not feel emotional loss after they mate and then go their separate ways?

The major difference between humans and animals, from a purely physical perspective, is that human beings have the most highly developed prefrontal cortex of all creatures. We are not robots controlled by our brain hormones and sex hormones. Yes, the brain chemicals and their impact on our thoughts and desires are powerful, but we have the capacity to control our actions. Indeed, to be fully human, we must. Therefore, in the early days of

> "Sex was always a given and usually happened the first or second time we were together. I didn't care anymore. I felt dead inside and thought this is just the way it is . . . I felt lost and hurt."
>
> JULIE, 27

intense romance, we can, thanks to our prefrontal cortex, rationally think through the implications of the relationship and forego sexual involvement. We can encourage our adolescents, college-age students, and unmarried young adults to do this also. When individuals become involved in sex in ways that are casual, careless, or noncommittal, they are, consciously or unconsciously, attempting to separate sex from the rest of their personhood.

Human beings are more than physical beings with body parts. Human beings are not just mouths to eat with/lungs to breathe with/legs to walk with/eyes to see with/genital organs to have sex with. We are beings that function—mind, body, spirit—as a whole. This includes our personalities, our likes and dislikes, and our capacity to connect and integrate with others. Being fully human means integrating our bodies, our minds, our spirits, and our souls into a unit working toward the goal of discovering our purpose and living out that purpose on this planet.[53]

We have a responsibility to ourselves—to our health, our well-being, our future—and to the world, since each of us is part of a family and a community. Understanding this should encourage us, if we want to reach our fullest potential, to do things that stretch and challenge us, and may even seem unnatural to our natures: to forgo sex outside of marriage. But it is only when we choose and learn to do those things that we grow into mature, responsible adults.

Some of the greatest damage done by society's casual view of sex is the separation of the sex act from the rest of what we are.[54] Not only has this view lessened the enjoyment of sex, it has hurt us as humans in one of the most fundamental aspects of our beings: our need for connectedness with another. Because sex is the most intimate connection we can have with another person, it requires the integration of *all we are* into that sexual involvement—our bodies, our emotions, our love, our commitment, our integrity—for all of our years. If sex is less than this, it is simply an animal act. Sex of this type can make a person "feel" close to their partner when truly they are not. Sex devoid of relationship focuses on the physical and can actually inhibit the best kind of growth in intimacy.[55]

> "After breaking up with the boy I lost my virginity to, it was never the same. I was always looking for that same feeling and I just couldn't find it. My relationships got shorter and shorter and I felt worse about myself every time they ended."
>
> ANN, 31

HANDLE WITH CARE

Clearly, casual sex can have a negative emotional impact on an individual. The aftermath of these experiences extends far beyond feeling disappointed that a relationship didn't work out. If a sexually transmitted infection results, teens are likely to feel shame and embarrassment.[56] Sexual bonding is an intense experience—unconscious, yet very real. As new contributions from the field of neuroscience are made available, we know more about how the human brain and body are made to have meaningful connections even from before birth. When individuals have sexual relationships, they have involved more than a pleasant physical sensation and emotional response. Because of oxytocin in the woman's brain and vasopressin in the man's brain, connectedness and bonding do occur. Short-term sexual relationships may result in the brain's response with oxytocin and vasopressin, but they are more of a "quick fix" that do not qualify as the kind of long-term connecting the human needs for wholeness.

An individual who is sexually involved, breaks up, becomes sexually involved again, and then repeats this cycle is in danger of negative emotional consequences. A 2012 study showed that sexual activity with a nonromantic partner was significantly associated with both moderate and clinically severe depression.[57] People who behave in this manner are acting against—almost fighting against—the way they are made to function. When connectedness and bonding form and then are quickly broken and replaced with another sexual relationship, it seems to cause damage to the brain's natural connecting or bonding mechanism.[58]

> "I was so naïve he said we wouldn't go all the way but he kept pushing and we finally did it. Now I care about him but am angry at him all at the same time. I don't know if I can ever fully trust him again."
>
> GINA, 18

The cycle of repeatedly breaking relationships is triggered (at least in part) by the "addicting" nature of sex, which, in turn, produces more "addiction." Individuals may become hooked on having sex, but they cannot immediately feel or understand the consequences of this lifestyle and these sexual relations and how they are molding their brains.

REGRETS

Even though a teen made a conscious decision to have sex, they still may have regrets. In annual surveys conducted by the National Campaign to Prevent Teen Pregnancy (NCPTP), now called Power to Decide, the majority of high school students consistently report that they think all high school students should hear a strong abstinence message in the classroom and throughout society.[59] Surprisingly, this view is supported by many students who have experienced sex, since we know that nearly three-fourths of them have been sexually active by graduation. High schoolers' regrets over not remaining abstinent are further evidenced by another finding of the NCPTP: 67 percent of teen girls aged twelve through nineteen and 53 percent of teen boys aged twelve through nineteen who have had sex reported that they wish they had waited.[60]

These short-term, damaging, and often regretted relationships undermine the purpose of bonding hormones such as oxytocin and vasopressin and the purpose of the brain, compounding the excitement of sex by producing dopamine. These physical processes, within the context of marriage, contribute to a fuller life, to our purpose as members of family and community, to our achievement of personal goals, and to our happiness. Sex outside of the appropriate circumstances distorts the reason we have those brain responses and often negatively alters the course of our lives.

> "I see what sex has done to some of my friends and their relationships. I know although I am tempted now, that my choice to say no will protect my heart and my body for the future. I try to remember that as I try to make good choices."
>
> **LAURA, 16**

BUT NOT THE END OF THE STORY

Many people by now realize they (or their children or their friends) have been caught in the cycle of broken relationships or a compulsion to continue sexual relationships that are harmful or even destructive. They may be experiencing the residue of problems from past behaviors and feel discouraged. However, the human spirit is strong, and no one should feel he or she cannot change or find a way out of the cycle. It may be a spiritual rebirth. It may be a firm decision and a strong will. It may be counseling. It may be committing to a group that agrees to help each other be accountable in their battle with sexual addiction or other behaviors.

While the brain of the fully developed adult is not as pliable as it is during the adolescent years, it is still moldable until death. Molding based on experience can continue to take place. Spiritual change, counseling, supportive peers, and group meetings that include encouragement for change are all experiences that can remold the brain.

Deciding to change behavior patterns is hard and takes courage, but it may be necessary for some people to do if they want to be the most fulfilled person they can be—and to accomplish the goals they desire and are capable of achieving.

Neuroscientist David Eagleman states,

All the experiences in your life—from single conversations to your broader culture—shape the microscopic details of your brain. Neurologically speaking, who you are depends on where you've been. Your brain is a relentless shape-shifter, constantly rewriting its own circuitry; and because your experiences are unique, so are the vast detailed patterns in your neural networks. Because they continue to change your whole life, your identity is a moving target; it never reaches an end point.[61]

Peter Eriksson of Sweden's Sahlgrenska University Hospital discovered that brains well into their sixties and seventies undergo "neurogenesis,"[62] or the development of new brain cells. This is encouraging information for individuals who are experiencing problems they desire to overcome—some of which may be traced to the way they were parented, some from abuse, but often from behavior choices they themselves made.

Some would say that problems individuals might encounter from past sexual activity with multiple partners or that started at a young age are natural and simply a part of life. Guys want to have sex. Girls want to have sex (and often agree to sex when they really want "love"). So people have sex whenever they feel they are "ready" because they believe that is simply the way they are made. However, just because a thought or behavior is natural does not necessarily make it appropriate or good.

Amy Tuteur, MD is an Ob/Gyn, the author of several books, and writes a blog called The Skeptical OB. In her book *Push Back: Guilt in the Age of Natural Parenting*, she writes: "Ironically, the belief that natural is better has arisen amidst a society that proves in every possible way that natural is NOT better. The average human life expectancy in nature is approximately 35 years. The average human life expectancy in first world countries approaches 80. . . . Simply put, just about everything that makes our lives cleaner, safer, more comfortable and longer is not natural."[63]

We remember things that did not come naturally to us, yet by working on that behavior we could accomplish it in such a way that it contributed to our life and our goals. Simple things such as staying in school, studying instead of cutting classes—it may not seem natural to attend class day after day, but the results allow us a greater chance at success in life.

So it is with sexual behavior.

Ultimately, it is easier and better for the adolescent and young adult brain to be molded and hardwired to habitually avoid destructive and life-limiting behaviors in the first place. This helps avoid the necessity of engaging in the difficult job of remolding as an adult. It also clears the way for a happier and healthier future, free of the emotional and psychological baggage that comes with a past filled with unwise decisions about sex.

TO **THINK** ABOUT

- Why isn't cohabitation as good an idea as it seems on the surface? Consider not only social implications, but what we know about the brain.
- Why can casual sex have a negative emotional impact on a person?
- How can we train ourselves to do what is difficult or what does not come naturally?

Chapter Six

THE PURSUIT OF HAPPINESS

As the scientific data cited throughout this book shows, physical changes occur in the brain as a result of our experiences. We have emphasized that behavior and experiences can cause our brains to form in such a way that good *or* bad habits develop—a process we have referred to throughout this book as "brain molding." We've also demonstrated that our brains can often "make" us continue either good or bad behavior as a matter of course because that is "who we have become."

But we human beings and our behavior are much more complex than that, and parents, guardians, mentors, teachers,

> "The hardest breakup I ever had was with the first person I had sex with. Fifteen years later, I still don't think I'm over him. I still dream about him and think about him and compare every guy since then to him. I'm married now and I feel like it's a threesome in my heart. He is still here. It is like he is a part of me and I still can't get over him."
>
> JORDI, 33

and anyone else involved in the life of a young person need to understand this. No matter what experiences a young person has had, adults who love kids and want their best can still be a powerful influence for good.[1] How do we get this information regarding the consequences of certain personal choices into the hearts and heads of young people?

In countless studies and polls, young people consistently say that the individuals in their lives who influence their behavior choices the most are their parents.[2] Even college students report similar levels of trust toward their parents.[3] Unfortunately, the only people who seem to be unaware of this fact are the parents themselves.

This truth offers a golden opportunity for parents—and mentors and others who have the trust and confidence of young people—to guide them toward constructive behavioral choices and away from destructive choices. Multiple studies continue to show that effective parenting substantially enhances adolescent sexual health. Parental connectedness with their teens, effective communication, and parental monitoring all have been shown to reduce risky sexual behavior in teens.[4]

Parents have numerous advantages over other adult role models (teachers, health care professionals, clergy/youth ministers, coaches) when communicating with teenagers. Parents can discuss topics that align with their values and can select the most appropriate time and manner for the discussion. Parents usually are intuitive about to their adolescent's particular personality and sensitivities, external circumstances, and maturity level, as well as their social, emotional, physical, and moral development. Additionally, parents will be able to provide their children with continued guidance and positive influence year after year.

Finally, parents know that sex cannot be separated from a larger, whole person interaction between two people. Sex is an intimate part of the love and relationship between two people. Sex is a part of the "stuff of life," including marriage, home, commitment, and family. Parents also know that the physical sexual relationship matures between husband and wife, growing in meaning and intimacy. This includes the physical exploration of each other's bodies because such intimacy requires a level of trust that takes years to blossom and flourish.[5]

Parents know that none of this

> **"What if they find out their dad and I had sex before we got married? And here we are telling them not to. They'll see that we turned out okay and draw their own conclusions."**
>
> **ERIN, 33**

is possible with short-term sexual experiences such as "hooking up," "friends with benefits," or even relationships lasting several months that are sexual in nature. So, parents know either through personal experience or intuitively what brain science clearly shows: that young people who are engaged in short-term sexual relationships are depriving themselves of authentic, fulfilling, and meaningful sex.[6]

WHAT THEY DON'T KNOW *CAN* HURT THEM

Integral to understanding the importance of providing guidance to young people is recognizing that the adolescent brain still has much developing to do. We have learned that until an individual reaches his midtwenties, he is not fully equipped to make the most mature behavioral decisions.[7] This does *not* mean teenagers are inherently incapable of making decisions or unworthy of trust and respect. Many young people make excellent decisions throughout their teen years and demonstrate impressive levels of maturity. Sometimes this results from the healthy guidance of parents. Occasionally, a young person is determined not to repeat the mistakes of parents who have made bad decisions. But the majority of adolescents are not as well equipped to make complex judgments as they will be after their brains have fully developed around the time of their midtwenties.[8]

If parents are unable or unwilling to provide guidance and counsel to their children, they are leaving it up to their children to make decisions that most do not have the capacity at this stage of development to make. When parents abandon their children when they need mature guidance the most, their children will often practice risky behavior with sex, drugs, violence, and so on—many times with disastrous results.[9]

GOOD PARENTING MAKES A DIFFERENCE

Research shows that "how" we parent our teens makes a difference in how our teens respond to our message about sexual health. Studies show that the most effective "style" of parenting is one that exhibits warmth and support, but that also sets high expectations of good behavior. Good parents are also involved in their children's lives, but they are not constantly hovering. Adolescents with at least one parent with this style of parenting report better well-being, higher self-esteem, and more satisfaction with life in general. When both parents in the home embrace this parenting style, their adolescents are even more positively influenced.[10]

Effective parenting includes monitoring adolescent behavior and using consistent discipline to guide behaviors. Studies show that this type of behavior guidance results in an older age for sexual debut, along with less alcohol and marijuana use and less truancy. Communication is another aspect of good parenting. In a home where communication is valued and practiced, there is a high association with success in adolescents.[11]

On the other end of the parenting spectrum are parents who are excessively permissive with their children. They are quick to respond to their children's needs but do not hold up high standards of behavior or achievement. Teens from these families have a higher frequency of substance use and behavioral problems. Additionally, teens whose parents are uninvolved in their lives have the most negative emotional and behavioral outcomes.[12]

IS THAT A FACT?

Equipped with the scientific information provided in this book, parents can confidently talk to their children and share these facts as a complement to the moral code and values to which a family adheres. Many parents have advised their children to remain virgins until marriage based on the values the parents have established in their home. Every parent needs to make clear to their children what the foundational values of the family are.[13] Far too many teenagers admit confusion or ignorance when asked what their family's values are regarding sex. Parents will be comforted and encouraged to know that in addition to the moral code to which they adhere, reliable scientific data supports their advice that their children reserve sex for marriage.

> "I don't want my kids to do what I did. I had no idea how my sexual past would affect the rest of my life. I worry my kids won't listen to my advice since they know I made very different choices, and in their eyes I seem fine."
>
> TORY, 36

Parents can confidently state that research supports, and personal experience confirms, that the best chance of a fulfilled and flourishing life is for young people to wait until they are in a lifelong committed relationship before having sex. This information can also make it easier for parents to initiate a conversation with their children about sex. Parents can confidently present facts, and not just their personal opinion, that refraining from sex until marriage is the best choice. Findings show that when adolescents perceive that their parents have a good understanding about sexual health, it has a positive effect on their attitudes and actions.[14] On this foundation, the generational argument from kids that "parents don't understand the modern world of sex" can in part be defused.

THEY ARE PAYING ATTENTION—NOW WHAT?

Parents who are aware of the high risk of sexually transmitted infections, nonmarital pregnancy, and the emotional pain associated with adolescent and young adult sexual involvement may become worried about these risks for their own children. They often ask what they can do to help their children avoid such problems. Here again, research provides direction.

First, parents should realize that even if they have had a conversation with their child about sexual behavior and its risks, the child can still often remain confused about their parents' expectations. Parents and mentors need to repeatedly reinforce the messages they want young people to understand.[15]

> **"Talking to my girls about sex is just so awkward. I don't feel like I know what to say; what is enough and what is too much. What if they ask me questions about my past? Then what do I say?"**
>
> **ROBERT, 39**

One conversation is not enough. No longer is it considered adequate to have "The Talk" at a certain age. This needs to be an ongoing conversation, year after year.[16] Daily opportunities present themselves for parents to segue into these conversations—such as commenting on sexual situations presented on TV programs or advertising.

Research also shows that when parents talk with their teens about sex, teens are less likely to be influenced by their peers' communications about sex, which have been linked both to permissive sexual attitudes and to risky sexual behavior.[17]

How much a teen is influenced by conversations about sex can depend not only on the information offered, but also on the quality of the parent-child relationship. When a teen perceives a parent's support in a conversation about sex, they are more likely to accept the information and act on it.

- Teens who see their parents as being interested in them and responding in a warm and caring manner are more likely to postpone sexual activity.
- Teens whose mothers disapprove of early sex and have a good parent-child relationship are more likely to postpone their sexual debut.[18]
- Teens who perceive that their parents have a good understanding of teen sexual activity report better communication with their parents regarding sex.[19]

Perhaps this data about the influence parents have on their children will help parents begin the conversation and keep communication open. Even when a child is resistant or appears uninterested, often they are actually listening and being influenced and guided by the parent more than anyone else.

However, it is critical for parents also to be good role models. If, for example, a parent smokes, it is ineffectual—hypocritical, even—for them to tell their child that it is unhealthy to smoke and then expect their child not to smoke. Similarly, if a single parent is engaging in sex outside of marriage, it is less likely that telling a young person to avoid sex until marriage is going to be highly effective.[20]

"BUT WHEN I WAS YOUNG, I . . ."

Most parents of teens today were either born into Generation X (1966–1976) or the Millennial Generation (1977–1994).[21] Gen Xers tend to be concerned about broken homes and they actually have less acceptance of premarital sex than the Baby Boomers (born 1946–1964) did. Question, parent—is this you? Millennials, on the other hand, demonstrate a high acceptance of premarital sex.[22] Many Millennials were raised in single-parent families and are not so concerned about broken homes. Or is this you, parent?

These are generalizations, of course, about entire generations, but they raise the question of how the attitude and behavior of the parents may influence the attitude and behavior of today's teenagers. Parents may want to identify which of these groups they fall into and evaluate their own attitudes about sex, cohabitation, and marriage, and consider what they are communicating to their kids or what they want to communicate to them. Perhaps a question to ask is, "Am I thinking about, and then communicating, what I want to communicate to my kids about sex and marriage?"

> "I'm afraid my kids will find out about some of the things I did. They'll see that I turned out okay and think that they will too."
>
> CAROLYN, 40

Since 1991, the teen pregnancy rate has continued to decline, but the US rate for births to teenagers is higher than any other modern culture.[23] On the other hand, sexually transmitted infections continue to rise, with numbers now reaching 20 million new infections each year.[24] Many parents of teens today may have experienced an unplanned pregnancy or an STD, but, even if they escaped those negative consequences of sex as teens themselves, parents still may feel hypocritical when advising their own children not to get involved sexually.

Obviously, the factors missing from both statistics are the unexpected psychological and emotional risks young people are taking when they are sexually involved. Such information has not been available in the past. Knowing this, parents must realize that—despite their own past choices—encouraging their children to wait for sex until they are committed to one person for their lifetime, is the healthiest choice.

IT TOOK A VILLAGE

Young people will often not have all the guidance and support they need if their parents are the only ones providing it. While parents are usually the primary and most important voices to speak into the lives of their children, teenagers and young adults benefit the most when not only their parents but also the society around them provides guidance toward the most healthy choices.[25]

One of the most effective programs for reducing teen sexual activity and teen pregnancy focused on just such a community-oriented approach. Although it happened

> "No one was interested in me before. I don't think I am as cute as some of my friends and I don't hang out with popular kids. I have to go all the way with boys for them to like me. I'd rather have sex than be alone again."
>
> RACHEL, 16

years ago, this event is a historic example of what can be done when members of a community are willing to work together for the benefit of its youth.

Carried out in the rural town of Denmark, South Carolina, the program enlisted all the influential groups in town to advise and guide their young people to avoid sexual activity. The program involved the schools, churches, business organizations, physicians, newspapers, and parents communicating the same message. The results were phenomenal: local pregnancy rates declined by more than 50 percent from 1981 to 1985. In contrast, the pregnancy rates for the surrounding communities rose by almost 20 percent over the same time period. By 1988, just three years after the program was discontinued, the pregnancy rate had bounced back up and even exceeded pre-program levels.[26]

The study was designed so that the entire community joined together to give their young people one message: sexual activity and the resulting pregnancies were not good for them or for their future. No one disputes the amazing outcome that benefited hundreds of young people through a community that united in helping their children make wise decisions. The sad ending to this story is that the example of success this study provided became mired in the vicious arguments that have swirled around the subject of sexuality education ever since. Had more attention been paid to this example of community-wide support and been emulated by communities across the country, many teens may have been spared from making unhealthy choices.

A CHANGE IN BEHAVIOR

We know that many individuals between age eighteen and twenty-four—and older ones too—have made mistakes in the past. So what happens next? Is it too late? Has the brain been so molded that there is no hope for a happy, productive future? For many readers, this may be a difficult question of life-changing importance. No one can change the past, no matter how much we would like to. Instead, each person must look to the future and decide how the rest of his or her story will unfold. Despite the effect of life choices on the brain, brain molding is not a permanent "scar." In fact, the brain is moldable into old age. Harmful habits molded into our brains can be changed with time and effort—and perhaps some challenges along the way. We will discuss this vital concept more at the end of this chapter.

For some, the next chapter in their life story may involve practicing what some have called "secondary virginity," by choosing to avoid sexual intercourse from now on until entering a life-long, mutually monogamous sexual relationship.[27] For others, the next step may mean avoiding compromising situations and creating new dating boundaries to maintain their virginity. Some people are left with the painful psychological scars of sexual abuse or manipulation that they must work through in order to be free of the emotional pain and even the acting out that may have resulted.[28] Each path presents challenges that can be difficult to overcome but *can* be overcome with commitment, persistence, and effort. Young people might wonder, with some justification: *What if my boyfriend or girlfriend can't accept changes in our relationship and chooses to leave? What if my friends see me differently because of this change in my life? Does this mean I will be left out of the fun and excitement of high school or college because I'm not doing what everyone else seems to be doing?*

MORE THAN JUST SAYING NO

The healthiest choice is to wait and experience sex in a lifelong, faithful, committed relationship, rarely accomplished except in

"All my friends at school are having sex . . . or at least saying they are. Virgins get made fun of. People think you are super-religious or weird or something. And everyone gossips about what everyone else is doing."

DEREK, 17

marriage.[29] For many people, that means making a drastic change in behavior now. For others, it means sustaining and remaining committed to a decision made in the past to remain sexually abstinent until marriage. In either case, it's almost never easy, even as people grow and mature, guide their own behavior, and make healthy choices. In the meantime, parents, guardians, mentors, teachers, and other adults must understand the culture, know the facts, and offer the healthiest and most effective help and support.

Research has confirmed what common sense would tell us. In a book published by the American Academy of Pediatrics, Dr. Kenneth Ginsburg[30] outlines the "7 Cs of Resilience" that help teens resist the pressure to engage in sex and other risky behaviors:

1. Competence—ability to handle situations effectively
2. Confidence—belief in one's own abilities
3. Connection—close ties to family, community, school, and friends
4. Character—clear sense of right and wrong and a commitment to integrity
5. Contribution—giving to the well-being of others and making the world better
6. Coping—possesses positive, adaptive strategies
7. Control—knowledge that choices and actions determine results

Ginsburg states, "Our goal must be to raise children who can handle the bumps and bruises that the world has in store. We need to prepare them to cope with difficult challenges and bounce back. We must help them find happiness even when things aren't going their way. We want them to develop deep, strong roots now so that their wings will carry them successfully and independently into the future."[31]

Here are some practical suggestions to offer young people that can help them avoid sexual entanglements, thus preserving their best chance of a bright future:

▶ *Find a good friend with the same commitment about sex.*

This is someone to share values, secrets, plans, and dreams with. Talk about fears and temptations, and lean on each other for strength. Many people find strength simply by being able to share their feelings with someone who understands and relates to them.

▶ *Write down your commitment to abstain from sex.*

Begin a journal that starts with your commitment to yourself to wait for any further sexual activity until you are in a committed relationship. You might want to collect motivational quotes or links to videos of celebrities who promote waiting. Write down your successes and failures. Learn what works for you.

▶ *Practice assertiveness.*

It can be difficult to stand your ground when friends, dates, or significant others pressure you into doing something you know is unhealthy and unsafe. Every person has the right to make decisions concerning their own body, especially when your health, future, and well-being are at stake. Take time to talk about your rights and how

125

you expect to be treated. Role play with a friend or an adult with different situations that may come up.

▶ *Make sure your values are known to anyone you date or grow close with.*

It is critical for someone who is attracted to you to understand the boundaries and limitations of the relationship. Making your views clear early on can lay the foundation for a rewarding relationship—or help you steer clear of one that was doomed to fail.

▶ *Don't get involved with someone who doesn't share your values.*

Talk about your plans for the future, and be clear about your expectations. If you are interested in someone who can't support your decisions and accept you for who you are, put a stop to the relationship and wait for someone who will.

▶ *Plan your dates to avoid difficult situations.*

Don't just get together in private places and see what happens. Find fun things to do with others or in public and keep the focus of the relationship where it should be. List ideas for group activities in your journal.

▶ *Avoid alcohol and drugs.*

Aside from all the other obvious risks, they will impair judgment and make tough decisions more difficult. Remember, it isn't always about your own judgment—your date won't be thinking clearly either. This is a serious concern in situations where a male is much bigger and stronger than a female, or in a place where there is no help nearby.

▶ *Introduce your date to your parents.*

Your parents will appreciate it, and it will communicate to the person you're dating what you value and how you expect to be treated. Parents can offer better support and guidance when they know the people involved. Parents can be more objective about a potential date than their children, as they are not susceptible to the trust and bonding processes already discussed in this book.

▶ *Limit the amount of physical contact.*

Decide how much physical contact you will allow between you and your boyfriend or girlfriend early on in the relationship and stick to it. Conflict often arises because of unrealistic expectations or surprises. Communicating the rules beforehand eliminates that threat and lays the foundation for a healthy relationship.

▶ *Avoid any exposure to or use of pornography.*

Make sure your friend is not looking at pornography privately. Never look at porn with him/her. Never be talked into the idea that looking at porn is in any way healthy or right. It does not help you with sex education or prepare you to be a good sex partner. Viewing pornography is harmful to your mind, emotions, and spirit.

JUST SAY YES

Young people are full of hope. They want to be accepted and truly valued for who they are. They need this in the context of authentic relationships with parents and other adults. These authentic relationships must be stable and loving. Young people intuitively know that "boundaries" mandated by those who love them are actually a sign of being loved and valued. Teenagers may push or even rebel against boundaries, but if they know they are loved and cared for by parents with whom they have a good relationship, they will usually not go behind their parents' backs and cross those boundaries.[32] They want relationships with adults and they want to be taken seriously by them.[33]

But teens are also fearful of being alone and not belonging. They fear that they may not actually measure up and that this fact will be revealed even though they may be a leader or perform well in athletics, academics, or other endeavors.

For that reason, it is important for young people to find outlets that help them remain strong amidst peer pressure and stay on the right course. Hobbies and pastimes are important for young people because their brains demand the dopamine input that comes with involvement in exciting activities. The healthy pastimes parents encourage will deter young people from participating in more risky activities that could be molding their brains to produce unhealthy behavior choices in the future (besides being dangerous to their physical health).[34]

> **"Sex doesn't make a relationship. You don't have to have sex to be in a relationship."**
>
> **TAMIKA, 20**

The suggestions listed below can offer the dopamine "high" that young people often seek and help them engage in healthy pursuits other than sexual activity.

Academics. The rewards of scholastic achievement are many: college entrance and other higher education opportunities, better jobs, the mere pleasure of learning, and personal formation. The emotional rewards that come with succeeding in the classroom can play a critical part in feelings of excitement, belonging, connectedness, and satisfaction.

The arts. Young people can find fulfillment in expressing them-selves through music, drama, painting, sculpting, or any number of other creative pursuits.

Athletics. Competing in team or individual sports provides a sense of achievement, healthy physical development of young bodies, and lessons in teamwork, problem solving, and self-discipline. Sports can also provide a positive environment for meeting friends.

Volunteer and philanthropic work. Meaningful work involves tasks and challenges that contribute to the home, neighborhood, and community. In addition to the accomplishment of completing a project, young people can learn that helping others is one of the most fulfilling rewards they have experienced. They will also learn skills that they may someday use as adults in their careers or every-day life.

Further, whether feeding the homeless, visiting a nursing home, aiding a disabled neighbor, or serving overseas on a youth group mission trip, plenty of opportunities are available for young people to be involved in doing good. Such activities can offer complex challenges and rich emotional rewards.

Spiritual development. Many young people find that practicing their faith is an exceedingly rewarding part of their life and that adhering to the tenets of that faith is directly related to other positive outcomes in their lives. Faith can challenge their minds, encourage discipline, deepen compassion, and connect them with others in a positive context.

LETTING GO

As we have noted, dopamine serves a vital function in the lives of young people. It makes them look forward to independence, to living as adults separate from their parents, and to starting the cycle of life again: marrying, having children, raising children, and then one day seeing their children grow and become independent as well. In part because of the dopamine effect, young people grow excited about future possibilities, even though what lies ahead may seem scary, uncertain, and can't be mapped out. Good parents understand that one reason they have been offering their children guidance is to prepare them to become contributing adults, independent and fulfilled.

"I never realized how nervous I would be about Angela's college years until we waved good-bye to her. Then I worried for weeks about whether or not I had taught her the right things, warned her about boys, and helped her to be ready."

EDDIE, 37

Without the stimulating influence of dopamine, young people might begin evaluating the pros and cons of moving out and decide that the safest thing to do is to stay home with their parents. After all, their parents have a house, a job with regular income, and have already figured out how the world works. So why leave? However, the dopamine reward contributes to a restlessness that cannot be satisfied by staying safe and secure at home.

Individuals vary in their readiness for this stage of life. Some are terrified, cautious, and hesitant while some can't wait for complete independence. However, almost all experience an anticipation on some level about the potential opportunities in this time of their lives.

This can be a scary time for parents too because, whether they know it consciously or just sense it intuitively, they realize that some young people get hurt in the process of becoming independent. Despite this, it is still vital for parents to gradually but finally let go.[35]

A WHOLE PERSON

As many parents know, no matter how loving and supportive an environment has been for a child, there is no guarantee that he or she will always make wise decisions or avoid problems that arise from poor choices (whether theirs or someone else's). These problems can limit their opportunities, keep them from accomplishing the things they have always dreamed of, and even affect them for the rest of their lives. A daughter, for example, may be the one out of four sexually active girls who becomes a teen mother and never finishes college.[36] Or she may get chlamydia and be one of the 15 percent of young women who become infertile and will never be able to become pregnant unless they can, later on, afford the expensive procedure of invitro fertilization, which even then does not guarantee pregnancy.[37] A son may be one of the 11,000 men who develops an oral cancer from an HPV infection.[38]

Conversely, no matter how bad the environment in which a child is raised, some will overcome the disadvantages of their upbringing and excel. Some children seem to be

> **"After I accepted the challenge to model the abstinent behavior for my teenage daughter, I expected to feel different. But I had no idea I would feel so clean."**
>
> **JENNIFER, 37**

formed from before birth to make good choices, to not be as influenced by their peers, by media, or by other negative influences. Some seem to develop a spiritual sensitivity that serves as a guiding light to their behavior.[39]

No matter how accurate or revealing new neuroscience is about how the brain functions, it does not "tell all" about the totality of human behavior. Human behavior is much more complicated than that. In truth, we are just beginning to scratch the surface about human sexual behavior. However, just because our knowledge is limited does not lessen the importance of more fully understanding and implementing what we do know!

We know that humans are not just a mass of muscle, fat, organs, and water. We will never be fully explained by scientific or chemical analysis. As researchers, we also do not mean to imply that people who are sexually abstinent until marriage have discovered the secret to a perfect life, or that people who have had sex before or outside of marriage have destroyed their potential. However, the most current research shows that people who have been involved in premarital and/or extramarital sex may have added complications to their future that can limit their chance of flourishing and achieving their potential without dealing with those complications at some point. This may mean making a determined effort to overcome these obstacles and may involve many sessions of guidance and/or counseling and/or coaching. Those who abstain from sex until marriage significantly add to their chance for avoiding problems and finding happiness.

TO **THINK** ABOUT

- What do parents have to offer their teens and young adult children?
- Is it possible to overcome past mistakes? How?
- The authors claim that "young people are filled with hope." Should they be? Why? What healthy goals, pursuits, and dreams can adults guide them to?

THERE IS MUCH more to the human experience than we could ever explain.

Chapter Seven

FINAL THOUGHTS

A quick glance in any bookstore, at a newsstand, on the internet, or at television programs confirms that Americans have a fascination with the brain. Books and articles abound with stories on Alzheimer's, IQ tests, headaches, and any other topic that relates to the all-important three-pound mass that sits between our ears.

This fascination with the wellspring of our thoughts and awareness that has exploded in recent years is due in large part to fundamental discoveries in our knowledge of the brain. Recently and increasingly, sophisticated studies of the brain have presented startling discoveries to researchers on questions that have baffled science for generations. These advances have allowed us to understand so much more about why we do what we do.

> "It wasn't easy, but I am so glad we waited. I'm healthy, I love my wife, and I just don't have the baggage some of my friends do."
>
> RICK, 30

The reason a book like this one is even possible is that neuroscience techniques for studying the brain have proliferated over the past twenty-five years. Relying on MRI technology and other scanning and imaging techniques, we now know much more about the brain than we did twenty years ago. With new technologies such as functional near infrared spectroscopy (fNIRS) being developed, we will learn even more. This technology will allow the person being studied, who will wear a special headband, to interact and move more. As a result, the research will provide better results than that of older technology.[1]

Of course, we aren't even close to knowing everything about the brain. In fact, the more we discover, the more we understand how complex the brain really is.[2] Countless questions remain unanswered. But we do know enough to inform people in practical ways about a great deal that is happening in their heads and about what to do with this new information.

In this book, we have discussed much of this abundant new data. We have focused on the information that applies to connectedness, attachment, addiction, infatuation, love, sex, cohabitation, marriage, and other issues related to our sexual behavior and sexual health. The data indicates that sexuality and sexual behavior are a vital aspect of our humanity. It is scientifically and behaviorally inaccurate to view sexual activity as though it has no impact on the rest of what we are as human beings: our emotions, health, habits, and nature. Sex is far too integral to who and what we are as persons to see it in isolation to the rest of who we are. We cannot separate the brain from the body. What our bodies do has a dramatic impact on our brains (and all that happens there, including emotions, and so on), and what we think in our brains will have a dramatic impact on our bodies and how we use them.[3]

THE DOCTOR SAYS . . .

Many decisions about sexual behavior directly affect an individual's physical and emotional health—both now and in the future.

Because of that reality, this book is designed to function as a caring and good doctor would—as one who is concerned about preventive medicine and wants patients to avoid problems so they can have the best chance for a healthier future with as few problems as possible. Such a doctor, though capable of helping a person overcome a health problem through medicine or surgery, is even more interested in helping the person avoid the problem in the first place.

For example, a doctor may see a patient who is drinking excessively. The doctor would likely tell the patient that while alcoholic beverages are not intrinsically harmful (except during pregnancy), excessive use can damage the body. In addition, the person who drinks excessively has a negative impact not only on himself but on those around him at work and at home. A good doctor, then, recommends appropriate and healthy use of alcohol according to the science about such behavior while giving the warnings about what can happen if such advice is not followed. This advice is not a moral judgment and is not a statement on the value of the person or their life choices. If the patient returns having made no behavior change, the physician does not consider it a moral failing and is not critical. The doctor merely reiterates the pattern for a healthy lifestyle and encourages it again without giving up on the patient or compromising what science says is the healthiest behavior choice.

In the same way, in this book, we have made recommendations for the sexual behavior choices that offer the greatest chance to avoid what could be life-changing problems. Some of these

> "My parents tell me not to have sex, but they never explain why. They just say that it's wrong and sinful. I'm sick of hearing the same thing over and over."
>
> KELLY, 17

recommendations may seem unrealistic. Some are surprising and run counter to the mindset of popular culture. Abstinence culminating in a lifelong committed relationship has long been perceived as a religious position rather than a lifestyle choice based on scientific reality.

But now, with the aid of modern neuroscience and a wealth of research, it is evident that humans are the healthiest and happiest when they engage in sex only with the one who is their mate for a lifetime.[4] Little data is available about those men and women who are widowers or widows or who have divorced after many years. It seems reasonable to assume that if they enter into a long-term marriage relationship, the same benefits accrue to them.

In the past, medical recommendations for sexual behavior were based on science that did not have the benefit of today's research and technology. MRI and other sophisticated brain imaging tools were not available until recent years. Consequently, societal recommendations about this important area of life did not account for the powerful and verifiable connection between sex and brain function; and they were based more on personal philosophy, prejudice, and ideology than any verifiable science.

Unfortunately, poor recommendations based on earlier shaky foundations still persist.

However, modern breakthroughs in neuroscience research techniques and the new data now accumulating are leading to a major change in approach to sexual behavior understanding and recommendations.[6] The science says that, generally speaking, the healthiest behavior, both physically and emotionally, is for persons to wait for sex until they can commit to one partner for the rest of their life.[7] Some will follow that recommendation. Others will not. However, we can now safely say that it is a suggested course of action based on scientific reality.

Moreover, as we consider all the data we have reviewed in this book, we are drawn to the conclusion that modern evolutionary theory about human sexuality is misleading. This theory can be summarized thusly: that human beings are (in the terms of those who propose the theory) "designed" to be promiscuous. The fundamental theory posits that men have sex with various women until they find the one with the best genes, and women have sex with various men who could potentially provide resources and security to father her child.[7]

The data presented in this book shows just the opposite. The most up-to-date research suggests that most humans are "designed" to be sexually monogamous with one mate for life. This information also shows that the further individuals deviate from this behavior, the more problems they encounter, be they STDs, nonmarital pregnancy, or emotional problems, including the possibility of making it more difficult in the future to develop healthy connectedness with others, even possibly with a future spouse.

And finally, as we have discussed, most young people (87 percent) think it is best that they be guided to abstinence and most of them (93–96 percent) plan to be married, with the average age of marriage being twenty-six for women and twenty-eight for men.[8]

NOW WHAT?

The science presented in this book and the conclusions drawn from it will have different effects on different people. Those who are single and abstinent will probably feel affirmed by what they have learned. Individuals who have been faithfully married for many years will perhaps be encouraged and understand more about their ability to stay together through all the trials of a lifelong partnership. Individuals who are living with a boyfriend or girlfriend, those who change sexual partners occasionally, and those who, though not living together, are in love and having sex may be enlightened by what they have learned.

Before dismissing what modern scientific research tells us about ourselves, because of where we are in life or because of our sexual decisions of the past, we encourage you to let this information enlighten you. For example, if you are in a sexual relationship that just seems "right" but your partner leaves or cheats on you and you feel used and misled, consider those feelings in light of what you now know about the brain molding of sexual involvement. If you are married but before the marriage, cohabited, or had multiple sexual partners in the past, accept the fact that the research revealed in this book shows that these past experiences may have produced brain molding that can then cause you a greater risk of failing to maintain a commitment to the marriage. Therefore, if cracks start appearing in your marriage relationship, take immediate action to resolve those problems. Such action may include marriage counseling, attending a marriage seminar, or simply talking to a trusted friend. Those who have been sexually abused in some way can use this information as validating their inner feelings that something is not right and motivate them to seek counseling and contact civil authorities when necessary. These are but a few examples of how this information can benefit your life.

> **"The hardest thing about encouraging my kids to be abstinent is looking in the mirror and knowing that I wasn't. They wonder why it is such a big deal to me. If they ever found out everything I have been through, they would understand."**
>
> **RICHARD, 41**

THE TIP OF THE ICEBERG

As we have shown with the most current science available today, over and over again, sex cannot be dismissed as an activity with little or no impact on the person as a whole. We know sex involves the entire individual. Perhaps the most damaging philosophy about sex in recent years has been the attempt to separate sex from the whole person. Neuroscientific evidence has revealed this approach to be not only false but also dangerous.[9] Popular culture would have you believe that young people should become sexually active when they feel "ready"[10] and that not to become involved sexually at that point in their lives will cause them to be sexually naive and repressed. As we've seen, the facts tell a very different story.

> "When we broke up I just ached all over. I didn't miss having sex, but I missed having him so much more than I ever thought I would. I still don't understand what happened to me."
>
> **CHERYL, 19**

Current neuroscience research shows us that the human mind is an astounding organ, one we will never totally comprehend. But beyond that, just as the brain is remarkably complex, it is even more difficult to fully grasp what it means to be fully human. There is far more to human experience than we can ever explain. Life is not just a collection of choices. Nor are we robots or mechanical beings who hopelessly get hooked on certain behaviors. And to think that we are nothing more than a group of "brain cells" or neurochemicals moved about by our environment is ridiculous. We cannot be explained by quantity, matter, or motion. However, we do know and understand some things about ourselves. This information, properly interpreted and utilized, gives us direction toward the most beneficial behavior choices. It gives us so much new insight into how to live in harmony with our innate nature and, therefore, to be more fully human. Living in accordance with this information gives us the greatest possible chance to enjoy our lives to the fullest.

The findings we present in this book are but the tip of the iceberg of what will be discovered about the brain in the next fifty years. But as we have said, just because we don't know everything does not mean that what we *do* know is of no consequence. The findings we report here are verifiable. The lessons drawn from the facts we present here are practical because they reflect the way humans are wired. The behavior recommendations are realistic and reasonable because they are based on reliable information of who we are and how we function best because of our human nature.

We look forward to more study of the human brain. Future findings will not only be exciting and interesting, but also help us understand more of how we function best because of how we are made.

Appendix

PORNOGRAPHY AND THE BRAIN

We discussed in the introduction to this book that we were compelled to revise and update it not only in order to provide the most up-to-date statistics, but also because there have been major changes in the sexual landscape of this country. We have already discussed several. One of the most startling of all is pornography. We do not have the space here to do more than highlight some of the basic ways in which pornography affects the brain and how dangerous it is to both adolescents and older people. And it is dangerous not only to boys and men, but also, increasingly, to girls and women.[1]

Many people who do not use porn become aghast when they learn just how prevalent and available porn is. For example, eleven porn sites are among the world's top 300 most popular internet sites. The most popular of these eleven outranks such popular sites as eBay, MSN, and Netflix,[2] and these sites are being sought out by millions of our young people. One nationally representative survey found that 64 percent of young people, ages thirteen to twenty-four, actively seek out porn weekly or more often.[3]

How bad can porn be? What are people seeing when they use it? Are the images like those centerfolds in old copies of *Playboy*? Far from it.

Common porn shows vulgar shots of men's and women's genitals. Also commonly pictured are grotesque acts performed by men toward women.[4] Not only that, porn today also shows vulgarity, physical aggression, and even rape and incest.[5] Such obscene and depraved behavior, especially the frequent portrayal of violence toward women, is the desired outcome of some of those who produce this trash.[6]

But how harmful is viewing porn? Terribly harmful. Porn viewing has become the primary "sex education course" for many young people.[7] If this is the primary way in which young people are being educated about sex, then how can they possibly have a healthy, mutually beneficial sexual relationship—whether in or outside marriage? In addition, we now know that viewing pornography leaves such an imprint on young (and even older) minds that it can become addicting.[8] The American Society of Addiction Medicine (ASAM) now includes sexual issues under it's discussion of behavior addiction. This inclusion is based on sound science. For example, the Max Planck Institute in Germany and other research groups have shown that patterns of addiction appear in the brains of those who view porn compulsively.[9]

Porn is such a powerful initiator of the brain's dopamine reward system that the desire for porn can override the cognitive ability of the frontal cortex to make wise decisions about behavior. Viewing porn regularly carries the risk of causing a person to view it more and more, and to desire more and more extreme porn, because the dopamine reward causes a stronger and stronger interest and overrides the person's better judgment to not view it. Included in this stunted judgment is, for example, that men learn from porn to treat women aggressively and that they are entitled to sex from all women.[10]

Further problems develop. Both men and women can begin preferring porn to sex with another human being because porn displays such exaggerated and novel sex.[11] One terrifying possibility as technology develops virtual reality (VR) to be more and more lifelike is that a human using VR will actually feel that they *are* having sex with another human—but doing sexual acts that are abnormally enticing because they are impossible for another human to do.

For further information we suggest the following resources:

- The Medical Institute for Sexual Health (medinstitute.org)
- The National Center on Sexual Exploitation (endsexualexploitation.org)
- Fight the New Drug (fightthenewdrug.org)
- Just1ClickAway.org
- Covenant Eyes (covenanteyes.org)
- ConquerSeries.com

ACKNOWLEDGMENTS

This book is the result of years of ongoing study of the emerging research regarding human sexual behavior by the Medical Institute for Sexual Health (MI). Throughout its existence, the men and women of this organization have been dedicated to this goal. *Hooked* would not have been written without the foundation of credible research, study, and data evaluation and collection produced by MI.

Lynne Lutz, PsyD, a practicing clinical psychologist in Carrollton, Texas, working primarily with women, has provided the powerful quotes found throughout the text. William Ruwe, PhD, a neuropsychologist working with the Neuro-Resources organization in Oklahoma City, Oklahoma, provided invaluable resources and review.

In addition to Drs. Lutz and Ruwe, the original, first edition of this book was the result of the work of the many competent physicians and scientists affiliated with the Medical Institute. It is impossible to name all of the wonderfully dedicated people who work or have worked there. However, acknowledgment of certain specific individuals who have laid the foundation for this book is a must. Gary Rose, MD, former president and CEO of MI and his assistant Kim French, Kate Hendricks, MD, MPH., TM; Curt Stein, MD; Josh Mann, MD; David Hager, MD; Anjum Khurshid, PhD; Jennifer Andrews, MS; Sheetal Malhotra, MBBS, MS, MD; Harold

Thiele, PhD, Patricia Thickstun, PhD, Leslie Romoli, Amy Campbell, Art Coleman, Jean Marie McLain, Alejandra Eckel, and Gladys Gonzales.

Jon Yarian, working with the Pinkston Group of Alexandria, Virginia, edited the initial version of this book. Without Jon, the valuable information we provide here would have been much more poorly organized and much more difficult to understand. We still value his initial work as we have worked, in this second edition, on the words he initially helped us with.

This second edition of *Hooked* is more than a mere update of the scientific research that is the foundation of the book. There has been a cultural shift in the sexual norms of our society since the original *Hooked* was published. These changes mandated multiple updates. Donald L. Hilton Jr., MD, FACS, a board certified neurosurgeon in San Antonio gave guidance on the appendix on pornography, a topic necessary to be discussed in this book. Dr. Hilton is an adjunct associate professor in the department of neurosurgery at the University of Texas Medical School at San Antonio, where he is the director of the spine fellowship and of the Methodist Hospital residency rotation. His research, publishing, and speaking interests often focus on neural mechanisms of addiction. Dr. Hilton is one of only a few authorities in the world on the subject of the impact of pornography on the human brain and the subsequent human behavior. We are grateful for the way he has shaped our thinking so that we may better inform readers on the topic of porn and its effects on the brain.

David Hager, MD, Don Nelson, MD, Jack Lesch, MD, and Richard Kiovsky, MD have each helped us update the information and references. Without their pitching in and reviewing the latest research, this project would have been much more difficult. The unflagging encouragement and support of our longtime past board chairman, Dr. Tom Fitch, has been not only appreciated but vital to our completion of this project.

The primary burden of this revision fell on the competent shoulders of our incredible Director of Science, Marilyn Henderson, BSN, RN. She has worked, worried, and sweated as she carried the burden of not only coordinating contributions from others who have been looking for updated science, but finding a majority of it herself. We thank her. The ones who benefit from the information in this book can thank her. She is wonderful. We would also like to thank her science assistant, Tya Johnson, who so ably helped Marilyn in what may look like a routine job but what indeed was a very difficult project. Amy Campbell, our Vice President of Finance, held down the daily workings of the Medical Institute, while we focused on the update.

Kevin Emmert of Northfield Publishing made this second edition happen. Without his guidance, patience, encouragement, and finally his expertise in editing to make all this coherent, it would not have become reality. We owe him our deepest and most sincere thanks and gratefulness for a job well done.

We also give big thanks to Pamela Pugh, who edited the first edition of this book, and the rest of the team at Northfield.

Financial support for this project provided by members of the Board of Directors of the Medical Institute and other generous donors to MI allowed this revision project to become reality. In particular we thank the DEW Foundation.

Though my (Joe's) wife died during the early phase of this revision, she loved this work and would have been an enthusiastic encourager during the entire process if she could have. I (Joe) loved my sweet Marion, and she loved me. I (Freda) love Lee and his tolerance of me for the hours I spent huddled over my computer, being blithely unaware of what was going on around me. This is just one example of the undeserved love that has been a core of the relationship each of us has had in our marriages. We thank you, Marion and Lee, with all our hearts and with all our love. Lee, you "hooked" me (Freda), and I am glad of it. And Marion, if you can hear me (Joe), your uncommon love for me did the same with me. Thank you.

JOE S. MCILHANEY JR., MD
and FREDA MCKISSIC BUSH, MD

Notes

Chapter 1: Let's Talk Sex

1. National Institutes of Health, "Puberty and Precocious Puberty: Condition Information," https://www.nichd.nih.gov/health/topics/puberty/conditioninfo/default.
2. "Sexually Transmitted Diseases (STDs)," Centers for Disease Control and Prevention, www.cdc.gov/std/.
3. Ibid.
4. K. Paige Harden, "Genetic influences on adolescent sexual behavior: Why genes matter for environmentally oriented researchers," *Psychological Bulletin* 140, no. 2 (2014): 434.
5. Jan Pringle et al., "The physiology of adolescent sexual behaviour: A systematic review," *Cogent Social Sciences* 3.1 (2017): 1368858.
6. L. Kann, T. McManus, W. A. Harris et al., "Youth Risk Behavior Surveillance—United States, 2017," *MMWR Surveillance Summaries* 67, no. 8.
7. M. O. Ogunsola, "Abstinence from Premarital Sex: A Precursor to Quality Relationship and Marital Stability in Subsequent Marriage in Nigerian Society," *International Journal of Psychological Studies* 4, no. 2: June 2012.
8. Kann, McManus, Harris et al., "Youth Risk Behavior Surveillance—United States, 2017."
9. W. B. Wilcox and N. H. Wolfinger, "Men and Marriage: Debunking the Ball and Chain Myth", *Institute for Family Studies*, https://ifstudies.org/ifs-admin/resources/ifs-researchbrief-menmarriage-083117.pdf, accessed June 2018.
10. American College of Pediatricians, "The Teenage Brain: Under Construction," May 2016 http://www.acpeds.org/the-college-speaks/position-statements/parenting-issues/the-teenage-brain-under-construction.
11. Frances E. Jensen, *The Teenage Brain* (New York: Harper Collins, 2015).

Chapter 2: Meet the Brain

1. J. Mendle, J. Ferrero, S. R. Moore, and K.P. Harden, "Depression and Adolescent Sexual Activity in Romantic and Nonromantic Relational Contexts: A Genetically-Informative Sibling Comparison," *Journal of Abnormal Psychology* 122, no. 1 (2013): 51–63. H. Savioja, M. Helminen, S. Frojd et al., "Sexual experience and self-reported depression across the adolescent years," *Health Psychology and Behavioral Medicine* 3, no. 1 (2015).
2. Mark Regnerus and Jeremy Uecker, *Premarital Sex in America: How Young Americans Meet, Mate, and Think about Marrying* (Oxford: Oxford University Press, 2011), 66.

3. J. A. Hess and T. A. Coffelt, "Verbal Communication about Sex in Marriage: Patterns of Language Use and Its Connection with Relational Outcomes," *Journal of Sex Research* 49.6 (2012): 603–12.
4. Regnerus and Uecker, *Premarital Sex in America*, 81.
5. Frances E. Jensen, *The Teenage Brain* (New York: Harper Collins Publishers, 2015).
6. G. J. O. Fletcher, J. A. Simpson, L. Campbell, and N. C. Overall, "Pair-Bonding, Romantic Love, and Evolution: The Curious Case of *Homo sapiens*," *Perspectives on Psychological Science* 10, no. 1 (2015): 20–36.
7. Bryan Kolb and Robbin Gibb, "Brain Plasticity and Behaviour in the Developing Brain," *Can Acad Child Adolesc Psychiatry* 20, no. 4 (Nov. 2011): 265–76. Markus Butz and Arjen Van Ooyen, "A Simple Rule for Dendritic Spine and Axonal Bouton Formation Can Account for Cortical Reorganization after Focal Retinal Lesions," *PLOS One Computational Biology* 9, no. 10 (October 2013).
8. Jensen, *The Teenage Brain*, 48.
9. Kolb and Gibb, "Brain Plasticity and Behaviour in the Developing Brain," 265–76.
10. Ibid.
11. Ibid.
12. Jensen, *The Teenage Brain*, 70.
13. Ibid., 54.
14. S. J. Blakemore and T. W. Robbins, "Decision-making in the adolescent brain," *Nature Neuroscience* 15, no. 9 (Sept. 2012).
15. Jensen, *The Teenage Brain*, 103–104.
16. Ibid., 114.
17. Ibid., 108.
18. Ibid.
19. Ibid., 109.
20. Ibid., 111.
21. Fletcher, Simpson, Campbell, and Overall, "Pair-Bonding, Romantic Love, and Evolution," 20–36.
22. Tiffany M. Love, "Oxytocin, Motivation and the Role of Dopamine," *Pharmacology Biochemistry and Behavior* 119 (April 2014): 49–60.
23. Ibid.
24. M. A. Whisman and D. K. Snyder, "Sexual Infidelity in a National Survey of American Women: Differences in Prevalence and Correlates as a Function of Method of Assessment," *Journal of Family Psychology* 21, no. 2 (2007): 147–54.
25. W. B. Wilcox, J. R. Anderson, W. Doherty et al., "Why Marriage Matters, Third Edition: Thirty Conclusions from the Social Sciences" (New York: Institute for American Values National Marriage Project, 2011).
26. R. Hurlemann and D. Scheele, "Dissecting the Role of Oxytocin in the Formation and Loss of Social Relationships," *Biological Psychiatry* 79 (Feb. 2016):185–93.
27. Fletcher, Simpson, Campbell, and Overall, "Pair-Bonding, Romantic Love, and Evolution," 20–36. Hurlemann and Scheele, "Dissecting the Role of Oxytocin in the Formation and Loss of Social Relationships,"185–93. K. A. Young, K. L. Gobrogge, Y. Liu, and Z. Wang, "The Neurobiology of Pair Bonding: Insights from a Socially Monogamous Rodent," *Front Neuroendocrinology* 32, no. 1 (Jan.

2011): 53–69. Z. V. Johnson and L. J. Young, "Neurobiological mechanisms of social attachment and pair bonding," *Current Opinion in Behavioral Sciences* 3 (June 2015): 38–44.

28. I. Schneiderman, O. Zagoory-Sharon, J. F. Leckman, and R. Feldman, "Oxytocin during the initial stages of romantic attachment: Relations to couples' interactive reciprocity," *Psychoneuroendocrinology* 37, no. 8 (Aug. 2012): 1277–85. A. Meyer-Lindenberg, G. Domes, P. Kirsch, and M. Heinrichs, "Oxytocin and vasopressin in the human brain: social neuropeptides for translational medicine," *Nature Reviews Neuroscience* 12 (Sept. 2011): 524–38.

29. Fletcher, Simpson, Campbell, and Overall, "Pair-Bonding, Romantic Love, and Evolution," 20–36. L. Brizendine, *The Female Brain* (New York: Broadway, 2006), 68.

30. Hurlemann and Scheele, "Dissecting the Role of Oxytocin in the Formation and Loss of Social Relationships," 185–93. P. Sun, A. S. Smith, K. Lei et al., "Breaking bonds in male prairie vole: Long-term effects on emotional and social behavior, physiology, and neurochemistry," *Behavioural Brain Research*. 15:265 (May 2014): 22–31.

31. Young, Gobrogge, Liu, and Wang, "The Neurobiology of Pair Bonding," 53–69.

32. C. F. Zink and A. Meyer-Lindenberg, "Human Neuroimaging of Oxytocin and Vasopressin in Social Cognition," *Hormones and Behavior* 61, no. 3 (March 2012): 400–409.

33. Young, Gobrogge, Liu, and Wang, "The Neurobiology of Pair Bonding," 53–69.

34. Jensen, *The Teenage Brain*, 107.

35. H. M. Alvare, "Saying 'Yes' Before Saying 'I Do': Premarital Sex and Cohabitation as a Piece of the Divorce Puzzle," *Notre Dame Journal of Law, Ethics & Public Policy* 18, no. 1 Symposium on Marriage and the Law (2012).

36. Regnerus and Uecker, *Premarital Sex in America*, 157.

37. T. D. Wyatt, "The search for human pheromones: the lost decades and the necessity of returning to first principles," *The Royal Society Publishing*, Dec. 2014, http://rspb.royalsocietypublishing.org/content/royprsb/282/1804/20142994.full.pdf.

38. T. Mostafa, G. E. Khouly, and A. Hassan, "Pheromones in sex and reproduction: Do they have a role in humans?" *Journal of Advanced Research* 3 (2012): 1–9. Wyatt, "The search for human pheromones."

39. Hongwen Song et al., "Love-related changes in the brain: a resting-state functional magnetic resonance imaging study," *Frontiers in Human Neuroscience* 9 (2015): 71.

40. Regnerus and Uecker, *Premarital Sex in America*, 152.

Chapter 3: The Developing Brain and Sex

1. S. J. Blakemore, "Imaging Brain Development: The Adolescent Brain," *NeuroImage* 61 (2012): 397–406.

2. Jack Bloomaert, "What is the purpose of a PET scan and a FMRI scan?" https://quora.com. Matthew D. Lieberman, *Social: Why Our Brains Are Wired to Connect* (New York: Crown Publishing, 2013).

3. Z. Petanjek, M. Judas, G. Simic et al., "Extraordinary neoteny of synaptic spines in the human prefrontal cortex," *Proceedings of the National Academy of Sciences of the United States of America*, 2011, PMCID: PMC3156171.

4. Frances E. Jensen, *The Teenage Brain* (New York: Harper Collins Publishers, 2015), 24–38.
5. Matthew Dahlitz, "Prefrontal Cortex," The Science of Psychotherapy, January 4, 2017, https://www.thescienceofpsychotherapy.com/prefrontal-cortex/.
6. Jensen, *The Teenage Brain*, 60.
7. Petanjek, Judas, Simic et al., "Extraordinary neoteny of synaptic spines in the human prefrontal cortex."
8. Ibid.
9. D. Romer, "Adolescent Risk Taking, Impulsivity, and Brain Development: Implications for Prevention," *Developmental Psychobiology* 52.3 (2010): 263–76, https://www.ncbi.nlm.nih.gov/pmc/articles/PMC3445337/.
10. Lieberman, *Social*, 241–56.
11. Alan N. Schore, *Affect Dysregulation and Disorders of the Self: The Neurobiology of Emotional Development* (New York: W. W. Norton & Co., 2003).
12. Lieberman, *Social*, 237.
13. E. L. Ardiel and C. H. Rankin, "The Importance of Touch in Development," *Pediatric Child Health* 15, no. 3 (2010): 153–56.
14. Lieberman, *Social*, 101–78.
15. Ibid., 132–33.
16. Ibid., 180–238.
17. Ibid., 241–56.
18. Helen Fisher, *Anatomy of Love: A Natural History of Mating, Marriage, and Why We Stray,* revised and updated (New York: W. W. Norton & Co., 2016), 23.
19. Mark Regnerus and Jeremy Uecker, *Premarital Sex in America: How Young Americans Meet, Mate, and Think about Marrying* (Oxford: Oxford University Press, 2011), 23.
20. Ibid., 145.
21. Ibid., 194.
22. S. Ortigue, F. Bianchi-Demicheli, N. Patel et al., "Neuroimaging of Love: fMRI Meta-Analysis Evidence toward New Perspectives in Sexual Medicine," *The Journal of Sexual Medicine* 7 (2010): 3541–52.
23. Fisher, *Anatomy of Love*, 21–23.
24. Ibid., 41.
25. Ibid., 26.
26. B. P. Acevedo, A. Aron, H. E. Fisher, and L. L. Brown, "Neural Correlates of Long-term Intense Romantic Love," *Oxford University Press SCAN* 7 (2012): 145–59.
27. Regnerus and Uecker, *Premarital Sex in America*, 136–39.
28. Ibid., 262.
29. Fisher, *Anatomy of Love*, 21.
30. Regnerus and Uecker, *Premarital Sex in America*, 180, 197, 202.
31. Fisher, *Anatomy of Love*, 39.
32. Kiecolt-Glaser et al., "Psychoneuroimmunology: Psychological Influences on Immune Function and Health," *Journal of Consulting and Clinical Psychology* 70, no. 3 (2002): 537–47.
33. R. J. Waldinger and M. S. Schulz, "What's Love Got To Do With It?: Social Functioning, Perceived Health, and Daily Happiness in Married Octogenarians," *Psychology and Aging* 25, no. 2 (June 2010): 422–31.

34. Fisher, *Anatomy of Love*, 303.
35. Regnerus and Uecker, *Premarital Sex in America*, 106.
36. Ibid., 61.
37. Ibid., 90.
38. Ibid., 77.
39. Ibid., 176.
40. Ortigue, Bianchi-Demicheli, Patel et al., "Neuroimaging of Love," 3541–52.
41. Louise Madill, "Sexual Abuse: The Healing Journey," *Focus on the Family*, 2010, https://www.focusonthefamily.ca/content/sexual-abuse-the-healing-journey.
42. Concept Systems, Inc., "Teen Dating Relationships: Understanding and Comparing Youth and Adult Conceptualizations, Final Report," *U.S. Department of Justice*, Document No. 248464, October 2014.
43. Ortigue, Bianchi-Demicheli, Patel et al., "Neuroimaging of Love," 3541–52.
44. Fletcher, Simpson, Campbell, and Overall, "Pair-Bonding, Romantic Love, and Evolution," 20–36.
45. Regnerus and Uecker, *Premarital Sex in America*, 194.
46. Z. V. Johnson and L. J. Young, "Neurobiological mechanisms of social attachment and pair bonding," *Current Opinion in Behavioral Sciences* 3 (June 2015): 38–44.
47. H. Savioja, M. Helminen, S. Frojd et al., "Sexual experience and self-reported depression across the adolescent years," *Health Psychology and Behavioral Medicine* 3 (2015).
48. Regnerus and Uecker, *Premarital Sex in America*, 201.
49. Madill, "Sexual Abuse: The Healing Journey."
50. L. M. Diamond and J. A. Dickenson, "The Neuroimaging of Love and Desire: Review and Future Directions," *Clinical Neuropsychiatry* 9, no. 1 (2012): 39–46.
51. Regnerus and Uecker, *Premarital Sex in America*, 72.
52. Ibid., 26, 72.
53. T. M. Love, "Oxytocin, Motivation and the Role of Dopamine," *Pharmacology Biochemistry and Behavior* 119 (April 2014): 49–60.
54. Romer, "Adolescent Risk Taking, Impulsivity, and Brain Development," 263–76.
55. Fisher, *Anatomy of Love*, 156.
56. Power to Decide (formerly The National Campaign to Prevent Teen and Unplanned Pregnancy), "Survey Says: Parent Power" (2016).

Chapter 4: Baggage Claim

1. Jean M. Twenge, Ryne A. Sherman, and Brooke E. Wells, "Changes in American Adults' Sexual Behavior and Attitudes, 1972–2012," *Archives of Sexual Behavior*, May 2015.
2. Office of Adolescent Health, "Adolescent Development and Contraceptive Use" HHS.gov, September 12, 2016, www.hhs.gov/ash/oah/adolescent-development/reproductive-health-and-teen-pregnancy/contraceptive-use/index.html. Sunil Kumar, "Emotional Maturity of Adolescent Students in Relation to Their Family Relationship," International Science Congress Association, *International Research Journal of Social Sciences* 3, no. 3 (March 2014): 6–8, http://www.isca.in/IJSS/Archive/v3/i3/2.ISCA-IRJSS-2013-173.pdf. Barbara A. Oudekerk, Lucy A.

Guarnera, and N. Dickon Reppucci, "Older opposite-sex romantic partners, sexual risk, and victimization in adolescence," *Child Abuse & Neglect* 38.7 (2014): 1238–48.

3. Kenneth J. Rothman et al., "Volitional Determinants and Age-Related Decline in Fecundability: A General Population Prospective Cohort Study in Denmark," *Fertility and Sterility* 99, no. 7 (2013): 1958–64. July 25, 2018, https://www.ncbi .nlm.nih.gov/pmc/articles/PMC3672329/.

4. Centers for Disease Control and Prevention, "Youth Risk Behavior Surveillance—United States, 2017," *MMWR Surveillance Summary* 67, no. 8 (2018).

5. Ibid.

6. American College Health Association—National College Health Assessment II: Reference Group Executive Summary Spring 2017 (Hanover, MD: American College Health Association, 2017).

7. Amy J. Rauer et al., "Romantic Relationship Patterns in Young Adulthood and Their Developmental Antecedents," *Developmental Psychology* 49, no. 11 (2013).

8. Mindy E. Scott et al., "Risky Adolescent Sexual Behaviors and Reproductive Health in Young Adulthood," *Perspectives on Sexual and Reproductive Health* 43, no. 2 (2011): 110–18, JSTOR, www.jstor.org/stable/23048869.

9. Brianna M. Magnusson, Jennifer A. Nield, and Kate L. Lapane, "Age at first intercourse and subsequent sexual partnering among adult women in the United States, a cross-sectional study," *BMC Public Health* 15.1 (2015): 98.

10. Frances E. Jensen, *The Teenage Brain* (New York: Harper Collins Publishers, 2015), 54–55, 11–113. Helen Fisher, *Anatomy of Love: A Natural History of Mating, Marriage, and Why We Stray*, revised and updated (New York: W. W. Norton & Company, 2016), 39.

11. Freda Bush, MD, personal notes.

12. T. M. Love, "Oxytocin, Motivation and the Role of Dopamine," *Pharmacology Biochemistry and Behavior* 119 (April 2014): 49–60. S. Ortigue, F. Bianchi-Demicheli, N. Patel et al., "Neuroimaging of Love: fMRI Meta-Analysis Evidence toward New Perspectives in Sexual Medicine," *The Journal of Sexual Medicine* 7 (2010): 3541–52.

13. Matthew D. Lieberman, *Social: Why Our Brains Are Wired to Connect* (New York: Crown Publishing, 2013), 70. G. K. Rhoades, C. M. K. Dush, D. C. Atkins et al., "Breaking Up Is Hard to Do: The Impact of Unmarried Relationship Dissolution on Mental Health and Life Satisfaction," *Journal of Family Psychology* 25, no. 3 (June 2011): 366–74.

14. Ortigue, Bianchi-Demicheli, Patel et al., "Neuroimaging of Love: fMRI Meta-Analysis Evidence toward New Perspectives in Sexual Medicine," 3541–52.

15. G. J. O. Fletcher, J. A. Simpson, L. Campbell, and N. C. Overall, "Pair-Bonding, Romantic Love, and Evolution: The Curious Case of *Homo sapiens*," *Perspectives on Psychological Science* 10, no. 1 (2015): 20.

16. H. Savioja, M. Helminen, S. Frojd et al., "Sexual experience and self-reported depression across the adolescent years," *Health Psychology and Behavioral Medicine* 3, 2015. Centers for Disease Control and Prevention, "Youth Risk Behavior Surveillance—United States, 2017."

17. American College Health Association-National College Health Assessment II:

Reference Group Executive Summary Spring 2017 (Hanover, MD: American College Health Association, 2017).

18. Mark Regnerus and Jeremy Uecker, *Premarital Sex in America: How Young Americans Meet, Mate, and Think about Marrying* (Oxford: Oxford University Press, 2011), 139, 143.
19. J. Mendle, J. Ferrero, S. R. Moore, and K. P. Harden, "Depression and Adolescent Sexual Activity in Romantic and Nonromantic Relational Contexts: A Genetically-Informative Sibling Comparison," *Journal of Abnormal Psychology* 122, no. 1 (2013): 51–63.
20. Centers for Disease Control and Prevention, "2016 Sexually Transmitted Diseases Surveillance," September 26, 2017, www.cdc.gov/std/stats16/ adolescents.htm. Michael Davies, "Sexual Health News–Sexually Transmitted Diseases," SexualHealth: The Better Way to Test for STDs, www.sexualhealth .com/sexually-transmitted-diseases-may-affect-mental-health_n_1483/.
21. B. Albert, "With One Voice 2012: America's Adults and Teens Sound Off About Teen Pregnancy," Washington, DC: The National Campaign to Prevent Teen and Unplanned Pregnancy (Power to Decide), 2012.
22. Joe S. McIlHaney, MD, personal notes.
23. "Counterintuitive Trends in the Link Between Premarital Sex and Marital Stability," Institute for Family Studies, ifstudies.org/blog/ counterintuitive-trends-in-the-link-between-premarital-sex-and-marital-stability.
24. Amanda Kepler, "Marital Satisfaction: The Impact of Premarital and Couples Counseling," Master of Social Work Clinical Research Papers, Paper 474, 2015, http://sophia.stkate.edu/msw_papers/474.
25. "Sexually Transmitted Diseases," Centers for Disease Control and Prevention, December 8, 2017, www.cdc.gov/std/life-stages-populations/adolescents-youngadults.htm.
26. Centers for Disease Control and Prevention, "NCHHSTP Newsroom," Centers for Disease Control and Prevention, October 20, 2017, www.cdc.gov/nchhstp/ newsroom/2017/2016-STD-Surveillance-Report.html.
27. N. Wilson Chialepeh and A. Sathiyasusuman, "Associated risk factors of STIs and multiple sexual relationships among youths in Malawi," *PLOS One* 10, no. 8 (2015): e0134286.
28. Freda Bush, MD, personal notes.
29. Charles E. Basch, "Teen pregnancy and the achievement gap among urban minority youth," *Journal of School Health* 81.10 (2011): 614–18. "Teen Births," *Child Trends Databank*, 2016, https://www.childtrends.org/ ?indicators=teen-births.
30. "Why It Matters," Power to Decide, https://powertodecide.org/what-we-do/ information/why-it-matters.
31. Mindy E. Scott et al., "The characteristics and circumstances of teen fathers: At the birth of their first child and beyond," *Child Trends*, June 2012, Publication #2012-19, https://www.childtrends.org/wp-content/uploads/2013/03/ Child_Trends-2012_06_01_RB_TeenFathers.pdf. 1–6.
32. "Teen Pregnancy Prevention," National Conference of State Legislatures, March 12, 2018, http://www.ncsl.org/research/health/teen-pregnancy-prevention.aspx.
33. Ibid.

34. Jennifer Wolf, "U.S. Child Support Statistics," *Very Well Family*, June 4, 2018, https://www.verywellfamily.com/us-child-support-statistics-2997994.
35. Ibid.
36. "Morbidity and Mortality Weekly Report (MMWR)," Centers for Disease Control and Prevention, September 21, 2017, www.cdc.gov/mmwr/volumes/66/wr/mm6637a6.htm?s_cid=mm6637a6_w.
37. "Prepregnancy Contraceptive Use Among Teens with Unintended Pregnancies Resulting in Live Births—Pregnancy Risk Assessment Monitoring System (PRAMS), 2004–2008." Centers for Disease Control and Prevention, January 20, 2012, www.cdc.gov/mmwr/preview/mmwrhtml/mm6102a1.htm.
38. "Reproductive Health—Contraception," Centers for Disease Control and Prevention, February 9, 2017, www.cdc.gov/reproductivehealth/contraception/index.htm.
39. Ibid. "Contraceptive Failure Rates: Table," Association of Reproductive Health Professionals, www.arhp.org/Publications-and-Resources/Quick-Reference-Guide-for-Clinicians/choosing/failure-rates-table.
40. "National Center for Health Statistics," Centers for Disease Control and Prevention, February 14, 2013, www.cdc.gov/nchs/products/databriefs/db112.htm.
41. J. Reed, P. England, K. Littlejohn, B. C. Bass, and M. L. Caudillo, "Consistent and inconsistent contraception among young women: Insights from qualitative interviews," *Family Relations* 63, no. 2 (2014): 244–58. Casey E. Copen, Kimberly Daniels, and William D. Mosher, "First Premarital Cohabitation in the United States: 2006–2010 National Survey of Family Growth," *National Health Statistics Reports* no. 64 (Hyattsville, MD: National Center for Health Statistics, 2013).
42. Fisher, *Anatomy of Love*, 53.
43. "Children and Teens: Statistics," Adult Survivors of Child Sexual Abuse, RAINN, www.rainn.org/statistics/children-and-teens.
44. National Sexual Violence Resource Center, "Get Statistics," https://www.nsvrc.org/statistics.
45. Ibid.
46. Ibid.
47. J. Hopper, "In Most Sexual Assaults, 'Defense Circuitry' Runs the Show," Dec. 19, 2017, verified by *Psychology Today*, https://www.psychologytoday.com/us/blog/sexual-assault-and-the-brain/201712/in-most-sexual-assaults-defense-circuitry-runs-the-show.
48. Jim Hopper, "Why Rape and Trauma Survivors Have Fragmented and Incomplete Memories," Dec. 9, 2014, https://www.jimhopper.com/pdfs/Hopper_Lisak_Why_fragmented_and_incomplete_memories.pdf.
49. Miranda Olff, "Bonding after trauma: on the role of social support and the oxytocin system in traumatic stress," *European Journal of Psychotraumatology* 3 (2012): 18597.
50. Ibid.
51. *Invisible Children*, http://www.invisiblechildren.org/2017/12/29/child-abuse-statistics-the-best-resources/.
52. Ibid.
53. Ibid.
54. Ibid.

55. H. E. Walker, J. S. Freud, R. A. Ellis et al., "The Prevalence of Sexual Revictimization: A Meta-Analytic Review," *Trauma Violence Abuse* (Jan 2017): 1524838017692364.
56. K. Lalor and R. McElvaney, "Child Sexual Abuse, Links to Later Sexual Exploitation/High-Risk Sexual Behavior, and Prevention/Treatment Programs," *Trauma Violence and Abuse* 11 (2010): 159–77.
57. Tara K. Cossel, "Child Sexual Abuse Victims and their Families Receiving Services at a Child Advocacy Center: Mental Health and Support Needs," *McNair Scholars Research Journal*, University of Nebraska-Lincoln (2010).
58. Lalor and McElvaney, "Child Sexual Abuse," 159–77.
59. Ibid.
60. Committee on Health Care for Underserved Women, "Adult Manifestations of Childhood Sexual Abuse," The American College of Obstetricians and Gynecologists Committee Opinion, reaffirmed (2017), https://www.acog.org/Clinical-Guidance-and-Publications/Committee-Opinions/Committee-on-Health-Care-for-Underserved-Women/Adult-Manifestations-of-Childhood-Sexual-Abuse.
61. "Sexual Assault: Males," U.S. Department of Veterans Affairs, last updated March 23, 2022, https://www.ptsd.va.gov/understand/types/sexual_trauma_male.asp.
62. Lalor and McElvaney, "Child Sexual Abuse," 159–77.
63. Centers for Disease Control, "Youth Risk Behavior Surveillance—United States, 2017," *MMWR Surveillance Summaries* 67, no. 8.
64. A. E. Bonomi, M. L. Anderson, J. Nemeth et al., "Dating violence victimization across the teen years; Abuse frequency, number of abusive partners, and age at first intercourse," *BMC Public Health* (2012): 12:637.
65. M. C. Black, K. C. Basile, M. J. Breiding et al., "The National Intimate Partner and Sexual Violence Survey (NISVS): 2010 Summary Report, Atlanta, GA: National Center for Injury Prevention and Control," Centers for Disease Control and Prevention (2011).
66. "Risk Factors for Teen Dating Violence," Youth.gov, https://youth.gov/youth-topics/teen-dating-violence/risk.
67. E. Ortiz and A. Johnson, "St. Paul's School Rape Trial: Owen Labrie Sentenced to Year in Prison," Oct. 29, 2015, U.S. News, https://www.nbcnews.com/news/us-news/st-pauls-school-rape-trial-owen-labrie-sentenced-year-prison-n452386.
68. Jess Bidgood and Rich Motoko, "Rape Case Puts Focus on Culture of Elite St. Paul's School," *The New York Times*, August 18, 2015, https://www.nytimes.com/2015/08/19/us/rape-case-explores-culture-of-elite-st-pauls-school.html.
69. Ibid.
70. Ibid.
71. Ibid.
72. Ibid.
73. "What Consent Looks Like," RAINN, www.rainn.org/articles/what-is-consent.
74. Jensen, *The Teenage Brain*, 117, 115–24. Jazmin Camchong, K. O. Lim, S. Kumra, "Adverse Effects of Cannabis on Adolescent Brain Development: A Longitudinal Study," *Cerebral Cortex* 27, no. 3 (March 2017): 1922–30. S. W. F. Ewing, A. Sakhardande, S. J. Blakemore, "The effect of alcohol consumption on the adolescent brain: a systematic review of MRI and fMRI studies of alcohol-using youth," *NeuroImage: Clinical* 5 (2014): 420–37.

75. American Academy of Pediatrics, "Children, Adolescents, Substance Abuse, and the Media," *Pediatrics* 126, no. 4 (Oct. 2010). From Policy Statement. M. A. Terizan, K. M. Andrews, K. A. Moore, "Preventing Multiple Risky Behaviors among Adolescents: Seven Strategies," *Child Trends*, September 2011, Research-to-Results Brief, Publication #2011-24.

76. B. Albert, "With One Voice 2012: America's Adults and Teens Sound Off About Teen Pregnancy," Washington, DC: The National Campaign to Prevent Teen and Unplanned Pregnancy, 2012.

77. Ibid.

78. Centers for Disease Control and Prevention, "Youth Risk Behavior Surveillance—United States, 2017," *MMWR Surveillance Summary* 67, no. 8 (2018).

79. William Bradford Wilcox et al., *Why Marriage Matters: Thirty Conclusions from the Social Sciences: A Report from Family Scholars,* 3rd ed. (Institute for American Values, 2011).

Chapter 5: Thinking Long-Term

1. "National Center for Health Statistics—Premarital Sex," Centers for Disease Control and Prevention, June 22, 2017, www.cdc.gov/nchs/nsfg/key_statistics/p.htm#premarital.

2. Mark Regnerus and Jeremy Uecker, *Premarital Sex in America: How Young Americans Meet, Mate, and Think about Marrying* (Oxford: Oxford University Press, 2011), 192.

3. Frances E. Jensen, *The Teenage Brain* (New York: Harper Collins Publishers, 2015), 57.

4. Centers for Disease Control and Prevention, "Youth Risk Behavior Surveillance—United States, 2017," *MMWR Surveillance Summary* 67, no. 8 (2018).

5. C. E. Copen, A. Chandra, G. Martinez, "Prevalence and timing of oral sex with opposite-sex partners among females and males aged 15–24 years: United States, 2007–2010," *National Health Statistics Reports* no. 56 (Hyattsville, MD: National Center for Health Statistics, 2012).

6. "American Adolescents' Sources of Sexual Health Information," Guttmacher Institute, December 21, 2017, https://www.guttmacher.org/fact-sheet/facts-american-teens-sources-information-about-sex.

7. Centers for Disease Control and Prevention, "Youth Risk Behavior Surveillance."

8. Ibid.

9. American College Health Association-National College Health Assessment II: Reference Group Executive Summary Spring 2017, Hanover, MD: American College Health Association, 2017.

10. Ibid.

11. Ibid.

12. Alfonso Osorio et al., "The sooner, the worse? Association between earlier age of sexual initiation and worse adolescent health and well-being outcomes," *Frontiers in Psychology* 8 (2017): 1298. S. A. Vasilenko, S. T. Lanza, "Predictors of multiple sexual partners from adolescence through young adulthood," *The Journal of Adolescent Health*: official publication of the Society for Adolescent Medicine 55, no. 4 (2014): 491–97.

13. K. A. Ethier, L. Kann, T. McManus, "Sexual Intercourse Among High School Students—29 States and United States Overall, 2005–2015," *Morbidity and*

Mortality Weekly Report 66 (2018):1393–97. http://dx.doi.org/10.15585/
mmwr.mm665152a1.

14. T. Ha, G. Overbeek, A. Lichtwarck-Aschoff et al., "Do Conflict Resolution and
Recovery Predict the Survival of Adolescents' Romantic Relationships?" *PLOS
One*, April 17, 2013, https://journals.plos.org/plosone/article?id=10.1371/
journal.pone.0061871.

15. Thao Ha, "New Research: Keys to Understanding Adolescent Romantic Relationships," May 9, 2016, https://www.etr.org/blog/my-take-adol-relationships/

16. Regnerus and Uecker, *Premarital Sex in America*, 23–24.

17. Renee Stepler, "Number of US Adults Cohabiting with a Partner Continues to
Rise, Especially among Those 50 and Older," *Pew Research Center*, April 6, 2017,
http://www.pewresearch.org/fact-tank/2017/04/06/number-of-u-s-adults-
cohabiting-with-a-partner-continues-to-rise-especially-among-those-50-and-
older/.

18. Regnerus and Uecker, *Premarital Sex in America*, 201.

19. Ibid., 199.

20. Casey E. Copen, Kimberly Daniels, and William D. Mosher, "First Premarital
Cohabitation in the United States: 2006–2010, National Survey of Family
Growth," *National Health Statistics Reports* 64 (Hyattsville, MD: National Center
for Health Statistics, 2013).

21. Regnerus and Uecker, *Premarital Sex in America*, 176.

22. Ibid., 199.

23. Ibid., 202.

24. Copen, Daniels, and Mosher, "First Premarital Cohabitation in the United
States."

25. Regnerus and Uecker, *Premarital Sex in America*, 180.

26. Mark Regnerus, *Cheap Sex: The Transformation of Men, Marriage, and Monogamy* (Oxford: Oxford University Press, 2017), 164.

27. Janice Crouse, *Children at Risk: The Precarious State of Children's Well-being in
America* (Abingdon, United Kingdom: Routledge, 2017), 62.

28. Robert Froemke and Ioana Carcea, *Oxytocin and Brain Plasticity. Principles
of Gender-Specific Medicine: Gender in the Genomic Era: Third Edition* (2017),
161–82.

29. William Bradford Wilcox et al., *Why Marriage Matters: Thirty Conclusions from
the Social Sciences: A Report from Family Scholars*, 3rd ed. (Institute for American
Values, 2011), 18.

30. Ibid.

31. Regnerus and Uecker, *Premarital Sex in America*, 175.

32. Michelle L. Frisco, Marin R. Wenger, and Derek A. Kreager, "Extradyadic Sex
and Union Dissolution among Young Adults in Opposite-Sex Married and
Cohabiting Unions" *Social Science Research* 62 (2017): 291–304.

33. Wilcox et al., *Why Marriage Matters*, 18.

34. Regnerus and Uecker, *Premarital Sex in America*, 200.

35. Jesse Owen, Galena K. Rhoades, and Scott M. Stanley, "Sliding versus deciding
in relationships: Associations with relationship quality, commitment, and infidelity," *Journal of Couple & Relationship Therapy* 12, no. 2 (2013): 135–49.

36. Regnerus and Uecker, *Premarital Sex in America*, 23.

37. Regnerus, *Cheap Sex*, 1.

38. Owen, Rhoades, and Stanley, "Sliding versus deciding in relationships," 135–49.
39. Regnerus and Uecker, *Premarital Sex in America*, 202.
40. Ibid., 176.
41. Sharon Sassler, Fenaba Addo, and Elizabeth Hartmann, "The Tempo of Relationship Progression among Low-Income Couples," *Social Science Research* 39, no. 5 (2010): 831–44.
42. Ibid.
43. Ibid.
44. Wilcox et al., *Why Marriage Matters*, 18.
45. Ibid.,14, 15, 18, 23, 24.
46. Regnerus and Uecker, *Premarital Sex in America*, 170.
47. Ibid., 174.
48. Ibid., 82.
49. Ibid., 171, 194.
50. Ibid., 169.
51. Wilcox et al., *Why Marriage Matters*, 15, 20, 24, 41.
52. Regnerus and Uecker, *Premarital Sex in America*, 174.
53. Matthew D. Lieberman, *Social: Why Our Brains Are Wired to Connect* (New York: Crown Publishing, 2013), 247.
54. Helen Fisher, *Anatomy of Love: A Natural History of Mating, Marriage, and Why We Stray*, revised and updated (New York: W. W. Norton & Company, 2016).
55. M. Reynaud, L. Karila, L. Blecha, and A. Benyamia, "Is Love Passion an Addictive Disorder?" *The American Journal of Drug and Alcohol Abuse* 36 (2010): 261–67.
56. A. Passanisi, V. Leanza, and G. Leanza, "The Impact of Sexually Transmitted Diseases on Quality of Life: Application of Three Validated Measures," March 19, 2014, https://www.researchgate.net/publication/286165338_The_impact_of_sexually_transmitted_diseases_on_quality_of_life_Application_of_three_validated_measures. M. Balfe, R. Brugha, D. O'Donovan et al., "Triggers of self-conscious emotions in the sexually transmitted infection testing process," *Biomed Central*, Aug. 17, 2010, https://www.ncbi.nlm.nih.gov/pmc/articles/PMC2930645/.
57. J. Mendle, J. Ferrero, S. R. Moore, and K. P. Harden, "Depression and Adolescent Sexual Activity in Romantic and Nonromantic Relational Contexts: A Genetically-Informed Sibling Comparison," *Journal of Abnormal Psychology* 122, no. 1 (2013): 51–63.
58. Fisher, *Anatomy of Love*, 151–52.
59. B. Albert, "With One Voice 2012: America's Adults and Teens Sound Off About Teen Pregnancy," Washington, DC: The National Campaign to Prevent Teen and Unplanned Pregnancy (2012).
60. Ibid.
61. D. Eagleman, *The Brain: The Story of You* (New York: Pantheon Books, 2015), 4.
62. K. I. Erickson, A. G. Gildengers, and M. A. Butters, "Physical Activity and Brain Plasticity in Late Adulthood," *Dialogues in Clinical Neuroscience* 15, no. 1 (March 2013): 99–108.
63. A. Tuteur, *Push Back: Guilt in the Age of Natural Parenting* (New York: HarperCollins, 2016).

Chapter 6: The Pursuit of Happiness

1. M. A. Terzian, K. M. Andrews, and K. A. Moore, "Preventing Multiple Risky Behaviors among Adolescents: Seven Strategies," *Child Trends*, September 2011, Research-to-Results Brief, Publication #2011-24.
2. D. H. Hoskins, "Consequences of Parenting on Adolescent Outcomes," *Societies* 4, no. 3 (2014): 506–31.
3. K. L. Roach, "The Role of Perceived Parental Influences on the Career Self-Efficacy of College Students," (2010), *Counselor Education Master's Theses* 88, https://digitalcommons.brockport.edu/cgi/viewcontent.cgi?referer=https://search.yahoo.com/&httpsredir=1&article=1087&context=edc_theses. A. E. Hodge, "First-Generation College Students: The Influence of Family on College Experience," Department of Counselor Education, Counseling Psychology and Rehabilitation Services, College of Education, Pennsylvania State University, http://forms.gradsch.psu.edu/diversity/mcnair/mcnair_jrnl2010/files/Hodge.pdf
4. J. Potter, K. Soren, and J. Santelli, "Predictors of parental knowledge of adolescent sexual experience: United States, 2012," *Preventive Medicine Reports* 6 (2017): 94–96. C. M. Markham, D. Lormand, K. M. Gloppen et al., "Connectedness as a predictor of sexual and reproductive health outcomes for youth," *Journal of Adolescent Health* 46, no. 3 (Mar. 2010): 23–41. M. Y. Sutton, S. M. Lasswell, Y. Lanier, and K. Miller, "Impact of Parent-Child Communication Interventions on Sex Behaviors and Cognitive Outcomes for Black/African-American and Hispanic/Latino Youth: A Systematic Review, 1988–2012," *Journal of Adolescent Health* 54, no. 4 (April 2014): 369–84.
5. G. J. O. Fletcher, J. A. Simpson, L. Campbell, and N. C. Overall, "Pair-Bonding, Romantic Love, and Evolution: The Curious Case of *Homo sapiens*," *Perspectives on Psychological Science* 10, no. 1 (2015): 20–36. H. Song, Z. Zou, J. Kou et al., "Love-related changes in the brain: a resting-state functional magnetic resonance imaging study," *Frontiers in Human Neuroscience* 9, article 71 (Feb. 2015).
6. M. Reynaud, L. Karila, L. Blecha, and A. Benyamina, "Is Love Passion an Addictive Disorder?" *The American Journal of Drug and Alcohol Abuse*, 36 (2010): 261–67.
7. Frances E. Jensen, *The Teenage Brain* (New York: Harper Collins Publishers, 2015), 37–38.
8. Ibid., 278–88.
9. D. H. Hoskins, "Consequences of Parenting on Adolescent Outcomes," *Societies* 4, no. 3 (2014): 506–31.
10. Ibid.
11. Ibid.
12. Ibid.
13. Sutton, Lasswell, Lanier, and Miller, "Impact of Parent-Child Communication Interventions on Sex Behaviors and Cognitive Outcomes for Black/African-American and Hispanic/Latino Youth," 369–84.
14. A. Holman and J. K. Kellas, "High School Adolescents' Perceptions of the Parent-Child Sex Talk: How Communication, Relational, and Family Factors Relate to Sexual Health," *Family and Health Communication* 80, no. 5 (2015): 388–403.
15. Jensen, *The Teenage Brain*, 80–88.

16. Centers for Disease Control, "Talking with Your Teens about Sex: Going Beyond 'the Talk,'" https://www.cdc.gov/healthyyouth/protective/pdf/talking_teens.pdf.

17. Holman and Kellas, "High School Adolescents' Perceptions of the Parent-Child Sex Talk," 388–403.

18. D. Wright and D. Fullerton, "A Review of Interventions with Parents to Promote the Sexual Health of Their Children," *Journal of Adolescent Health* 52 (2013): 4–27.

19. J. Potter, K. Soren, and J. Santelli, "Predictors of parental knowledge of adolescent sexual experience: United States, 2012," *Preventive Medicine Reports* 6 (2017): 94–96.

20. Centers for Disease Prevention and Control, "Ways to Influence Your Teen's Sexual Risk Behavior: What Fathers Can Do," *Division of Adolescent and School Health*, November 2013, https://www.cdc.gov/healthyyouth/protective/pdf/fathers_influence.pdf.

21. The Center for Generational Kinetics, "Top 10 Gen Z Questions Answered," http://genhq.com/igen-gen-z-generation-z-centennials-info/.

22. J. M. Twenge, R. A. Sherman, B. E. Wells, "Changes in American Adults' Sexual Behavior and Attitudes, 1972–2012," *Archives of Sexual Behavior* 44, no. 8 (2015): 2273–85. https://link.springer.com/article/10.1007/s10508-015-0540-2.

23. J. A. Martin, B. E. Hamilton, M. J. K. Osterman et al., "Births: Final Data for 2016," *National Vital Statistics Reports* 67, no. 1, https://www.cdc.gov/nchs/data/nvsr/nvsr67/nvsr67_01.pdf.

24. Centers for Disease Control and Prevention, "Sexually Transmitted Disease Surveillance 2016," https://www.cdc.gov/std/stats16/exordium.htm.

25. D. H. Hoskins, "Consequences of Parenting on Adolescent Outcomes," *Societies* 4, no. 3 (2014): 506–31.

26. M. L. Vincent, A. F. Clearie, and M. D. Schluchter, "Reducing Adolescent Pregnancy through a School- and Community-Based Education," *The Journal of the American Medical Association* 257, no. 24 (1987): 3382–86. H. P. Koo, G. H. Dunteman, C. George et al., "Reducing Adolescent Pregnancy through a School- and Commuity-Based Intervention: Denmark, South Carolina, Revisited," *Family Planning Perspectives* 26, no. 5 (1994): 206–11, 217.

27. L. M. Carpenter, "Like a Virgin . . . Again?: Secondary Virginity as an Ongoing Gendered Social Construction," *Sexuality & Culture* 15, no. 2 (June 2011): 115–40.

28. Centers for Disease Control and Prevention, "Child Abuse and Neglect: Consequences," https://www.cdc.gov/violenceprevention/childabuseand neglect/consequences.html. C. A. Stappenbeck, W. H. George, J. M. Staples et al., "In-The-Moment Dissociation, Emotional Numbing, and Sexual Risk: The Influence of Sexual Trauma History, Trauma Symptoms, and Alcohol Intoxication," *Psychology of Violence* 6, no. 4 (2016): 586–95.

29. Mark Regnerus and Jeremy Uecker, *Premarital Sex in America: How Young Americans Meet, Mate, and Think about Marrying* (Oxford: Oxford University Press, 2011), 174–75.

30. K. R. Ginsburg, *Building Resilience in Children and Teens: Giving Kids Roots and Wings*, 3rd ed. (Elk Grove Village, IL: American Academy of Pediatrics, 2015), 24–29.
31. Ibid., 3.
32. D. H. Hoskins, "Consequences of Parenting on Adolescent Outcomes," *Societies* 4, no. 3 (2014): 506–31.
33. Ginsburg, *Building Resilience in Children and Teens*, 128.
34. Jensen, *The Teenage Brain*, 73, 237.
35. Ginsburg, *Building Resilience in Children and Teens*, 280–81.
36. Power to Decide (formerly The National Campaign to Prevent Teen and Unplanned Pregnancy), Teen Pregnancy in the United States, Washington, DC, 2016, https://powertodecide.org/what-we-do/information/resource-library/fast-facts-teen-pregnancy-united-states.
37. Centers for Disease Control and Prevention, "STDs & Infertility," last updated October 6, 2017, https://www.cdc.gov/std/infertility/default.htm.
38. Centers for Disease Control and Prevention, "How Many Cancers Are Linked with HPV Each Year?," https://www.cdc.gov/cancer/hpv/statistics/cases.htm.
39. D. Murphy, M. Barry, and B. Vaughn, "Positive Mental Health: Resilience," *Child Trends,* January 2013, publication #2013-3, *Adolescent Health Highlight*.

Chapter 7: Final Thoughts

1. Matthew D. Lieberman, *Social: Why Our Brains Are Wired to Connect* (New York: Crown Publishing, 2013), 302.
2. Frances E. Jensen, *The Teenage Brain* (New York: Harper Collins Publishers, 2015), 24–29.
3. Nan J. Wise et al., "Brain Activity Unique to Orgasm in Women: An FMRI Analysis," *The Journal of Sexual Medicine* 14, no. 11 (2017): 1380–91. Gerben B. Ruesink and Janniko R. Georgiadis, "Brain Imaging of Human Sexual Response: Recent Developments and Future Directions," *Current Sexual Health Reports* 9, no. 4 (2017): 183–91.
4. G. J. O. Fletcher, J. A. Simpson, L. Campbell, and N. C. Overall, "Pair-Bonding, Romantic Love, and Evolution: The Curious Case of *Homo sapiens*," *Perspectives on Psychological Science* 10, no. 1 (2015): 20–36. "Sexually Transmitted Diseases (STDs)," Centers for Disease Control and Prevention, March 31, 2016, www.cdc.gov/std/prevention/default.htm. Mark Regnerus and Jeremy Uecker, *Premarital Sex in America: How Young Americans Meet, Mate, and Think about Marrying* (Oxford: Oxford University Press, 2011), 181.
5. Fletcher, Simpson, Campbell, and Overall, "Pair-Bonding, Romantic Love, and Evolution," 20–36.
6. "Sexually Transmitted Diseases (STDs)," Centers for Disease Control and Prevention, March 31, 2016, www.cdc.gov/std/prevention/default.htm. Regnerus and Uecker, *Premarital Sex in America*, 174, 175, 243.
7. Helen Fisher, *Anatomy of Love: A Natural History of Mating, Marriage, and Why We Stray*, revised and updated (New York: W. W. Norton & Company, 2016), 47.
8. B. Albert, "With One Voice 2012: America's Adults and Teens Sound Off About Teen Pregnancy," Washington, DC: The National Campaign to Prevent Teen and Unplanned Pregnancy (2012). Regnerus and Uecker, *Premarital Sex in America*, 169.

9. Nan J. Wise et al., "Brain Activity Unique to Orgasm in Women: An FMRI Analysis," *The Journal of Sexual Medicine* 14, no. 11 (2017): 1380–91. Gerben B. Ruesink and Janniko R. Georgiadis, "Brain Imaging of Human Sexual Response: Recent Developments and Future Directions," *Current Sexual Health Reports* 9, no. 4 (2017): 183–91.

10. Regnerus and Uecker, *Premarital Sex in* America, 18, 58–62.

Appendix: Pornography and the Brain

1. National Center on Sexual Exploitation, "Pornography & Public Health: Research Summary," June 8, 2017, https://endsexualexploitation.org/wp-content/uploads/NCOSE_Pornography-PublicHealth_ResearchSummary_7-26-18.pdf.

2. J. Marciano, "Top 300 Biggest Websites: Based on Both Mobile and Desktop Data for the First Time!" *Similar Web*, July 19, 2016, https://www.similarweb.com/blog/new-website-ranking.

3. Barna Group, *The Porn Phenomenon: The Impact of Pornography in the Digital Age* (Ventura, CA: Josh McDowell Ministry, 2016), 41.

4. Ana J. Bridges, Robert Wosnitzer, Erica Scharrer, Chyng Sun, and Rachael Liberman, "Aggression and Sexual Behavior in Best-Selling Pornography Videos."

5. Ibid. Chiara Sabina, Janis Wolak, and David Finkelhor, "The Nature and Dynamics of Internet Pornography Exposure for Youth," *CyberPsychology & Behavior* 11, no. 6 (2008). *Sage Journals* 16, no. 10 (Oct. 26, 2010): 1065–85, http://journals.sagepub.com/doi/10.1177/1077801210382866.

6. Bill Margold, pornography performer, quoted by Gail Dines, "Pornland: How Porn Has Hijacked our Sexuality," (Boston: Beacon Press, 2010).

7. Chiara Sabina, Janis Wolak, and David Finkelhor, "The Nature and Dynamics of Internet Pornography Exposure for Youth," *CyberPsychology & Behavior* 11, no. 6 (2008).

8. *Your Brain On Porn* website. It provides a detailed list of the latest peer-reviewed papers showing harm, and also documenting the evidence for an addictive model for porn.

9. Donald L. Hilton Jr., Clark Watts, "Pornography Addiction: A Neuroscience Perspective," *Surgical Neurology International* (2011) 2:19. Simone Kuhn and Jurgen Gallinat, "Brain Structure and Functional Connectivity Associated with Pornography Consumption: The Brain On Porn," *JAMA Psychiatry*, May 28, 2014. C. Schmidt, L. S. Morris, T. L. Kvamme, P. Hall, T. Birchard, and V. Voon, "Compulsive sexual behavior: Prefrontal and limbic volume and interactions. Human Brain Mapping" (2016). V. Voon, T. B. Mole, P. Banca, L. Porter, L. Morris, S. Mitchell, T. R. Lapa, M. N. Potenza, and M. Irvine, "Neural Correlates of Sexual Cue Reactivity in Individuals with and without Compulsive Sexual Behaviors," *PLOS One*, July 11, 2014. D. G. Mechelmans, M. Irvine, P. Banca et al., "Enhanced Attentional Bias Towards Sexually Explicit Cues in Individuals with and without Compulsive Sexual Behaviours," *PLOS One* (2014). M. Gola, M. Wordecha, G. Sescousse, M. Lew-Starowicz, B. Kossowski, M. Wypych, S. Makeig, M. N. Potenza, and A. Marchewka, "Can Pornography Be Addictive? An fMRI Study of Men Seeking Treatment for Problematic Pornography Use," *Neuropsychopharmacology* 42, no. 10 (Sept. 2017): 2021–31.

10. Jesselyn Cook, "Inside Incels' Looksmaxing Obsession: Penis Stretching, Skull Implants and Rage. Thousands of 'involuntarily celibate' men in online forums are consumed by misogynist entitlement and a skin-deep quest for self-improvement," July 24, 2018, updated July 27, 2018, *Huffington Post*, https://www.huffingtonpost.com/entry/incels-looksmaxing-obsession_us_5b50e56ee4b0de86f48b0a4f.
11. Press Release, Karolinska Institutet, https://www.nobelprize.org/prizes/medicine/1973/press-release/.

Index

Abstinence
    happiness and, 123, 132
    teenagers' views of, 90–91, 109, 139
Abuse, sexual, 83–88
Activities for young people, 128–29
Adult guidance. *See* Guidance
Alcohol and drugs, 126
Appetite, 14–15
Assertiveness, 125
Awakening, 14–15
Axons, 25, 29

Behavior change, 19, 110–12, 118–19, 122–23
Birth control, 12, 83
Bonding
    in broken relationships, 66–67, 88, 108
    in cohabiting couples, 100–104
    during intercourse, 75
    need for inborn, 81
    oxytocin and, 33–40, 43–44, 108
    vasopressin and, 39–41, 109
Boundaries, 128
Boys, sexual abuse of, 86
Brain
    chemicals, tracking, 24
    decision making and, 20
    judgment and, 49, 115–16
    as moldable/adaptable, 27–28, 32, 38, 51–52, 95, 110, 123
    neurogenesis, 111
    neurons, 25–26
    neuroscientific research on, 21, 48–50
    overview, 43–45
    prefrontal cortex, 33, 49, 51–52, 105–6
    remolding, 110–12
    as sex organ, 24, 43
    sexual excitement and, 16
    support cells, 25
    synapses, 26–29
Breakups
    reasons for, 57, 65
    results of, 75–77, 107–9
Broken relationships, 66–67, 110

Children
    childhood sexual abuse, 86–87
    connectedness in, 52–53
    mirror neurons and, 54
    in stable marriages, 39, 63
Cohabitation, 100–3, 112, 120, 136
Commitment
    in cohabiting relationships, 62, 100
    premarital sex and, 83
Condoms, 12, 72, 80, 83
Connectedness, 53–56, 61
Connection, 26–29, 35, 52–54, 61, 63, 66, 76, 84, 107
Contraceptives, 12, 82–83
Cytoplasm, 25

Date rape, 84, 86, 88, 90
Defense circuitry
Decision making, 20, 65, 110, 115–16
Dendrites, 25
Denmark, South Carolina, 121–22
Depression/suicide attempts, 20, 77
Disease, 12, 15, 77, 80, 120–21
Divorce, 67, 79, 81, 101
Doing what is natural, 111
Dopamine
    addictive drugs similarity, 32, 74
    functions of, 29–33, 73, 109
    providing excitement/action, 30–33, 60
    "reward signal" action, 29, 32, 74
    risk and, 31–32
    role of in adolescents, 30–31

Effective parenting, 114, 116
Emotional intimacy, 104
Endorphins, 42
Estrogen, 14, 42
Evolution, 139

Friends with benefits, 98, 115

Gonorrhea, 80
Guidance, community-centered, 121–22
Guidance, parent/mentor
    impact of, 19, 114–21
    importance of, 66, 68
    reasons for, 92–93
    See also Parents
Happiness, 67, 97, 105, 109, 123

Harmonizing, 54
Health
    in close sexual relationships, 60–61
    in high-conflict relationships, 61
Herpes, 80–81
HIV/AIDS, 15
Home environment, 19, 63
Hooking up, 41, 98, 115
Hormones, 14, 19, 72–73, 105

Infatuation, 55–58
Infection
    disclosure of, 81
    potential, 17
    See also STDs (sexually transmitted diseases)
Infidelity, 102
Intercourse, 33–35, 72, 73 74, 98
Intuition, 57

Judgment, maturity for, 49, 114

Living together. See Cohabitation
Love, 56–57, 59–61
Lust, 62 65

Magnetic Resonance Imaging (MRI), 48–49, 54, 135–36, 138
Manipulation, sexual, 88–91
Marriage
    care of children and, 35, 92, 104
    oxytocin and, 35–37
    premarital sex and, 98–99
    providing stability/success, 35, 104–5
    relationship health and, 56, 63, 105
Mature judgment, 50–51
Mentoring. See Guidance, parent/mentor; Parents
Mindreading, 54
"Mirror neurons," 54
Molestation, 86, 97
Monogamous, nonmarital relationships
    characteristics of, 56, 100, 104
    risks of, 100
MRI (Magnetic Resonance Imaging), 48–49, 54, 135–36, 138
Multiple sexual partners
    age first sex experience and, 74
    high school/college students, 98–99

National Campaign to Prevent Teen Pregnancy (NCPTP), 91, 109
Neurochemicals, 28–41

Neurogenesis, 111
Neurons
    connections of, 25–26
    described, 25
    "mirror neurons," 54
    neurogenesis, 111

Neuroscience research techniques
    breakthroughs in, 24, 138
    MRI (Magnetic Resource Imaging), 48–49, 54, 135–36, 138
    recommendations from, 138, 141–42
Nurturing, 54–55

Oral sex, 17, 73, 80, 98, 99
Oxytocin
    action of, 34
    bonding caused by, 34–36, 38–39, 43–44
    dilemmas caused by, 39
    reasons for release of, 33–34, 37, 44
    trust built by, 37

Parents
    guidance/counsel by, 114–21, 124–25
    impact of on behavior, 114, 116, 119
    letting go, 129–130
    as role models, 114, 119
    "The Talk," 118–19
Pedophiles, 86
PET scan, 48–49
Pheromones, impact of, 42
Physical contact, limiting, 127
Power to Decide, 91, 109
Prefrontal cortex, 33, 49, 51–52, 105–6
Pregnancy
    cohabiting couples and, 101
    contraceptives/condoms and, 83
    out-of-wedlock, 12, 83
Premarital childbearing, 101
Premarital sex, 38, 59, 67, 78, 79, 132
Progesterone, 42
Promiscuity, 139
Puberty, 13–14, 19
PTSD, 85–87

Rape, 71–72, 83–86, 88–90
Rationalizations, 96
Regrets, 109

Relationships
    broken, 66–67, 110
    connectedness of, 52–56
    intact/stable, 35, 39, 62, 63
    marriages as, 60–61
    mature/immature, 59, 63
    parent/mentor guidance and, 51–52, 66–68
    stages of, 55–56
Remolding, 27, 110, 112
"Reward signal" action, dopamine, 29, 32, 74
Risks
    dopamine and, 30–32
    of hooking up, 98–99
    of premarital sex, 96–97, 98–99
    of short-term sexual relationships, 63, 66–67
    of substance abuse, 91
Rules, abiding by, 127

Security, 62–63, 139
Serotonin, 43
Sex
    benefits, 8, 15, 17, 60
    as connectedness, 52–55, 107–8
    defined, 15–18
    human vs. animal, 105–6
    love and, 56, 57–58, 59–60, 67
    as lust, 62, 65
Sexual abuse, 83–88
Sexual activity
    abstaining from, suggestions, 125–29
    as addictive, 12–13, 33, 75–76, 99, 108
    adolescent, ramifications of, 19, 80
    brain and, 16
    definition, 16
    high school/college, 98–99
    infection potential, 17, 80
    normalization of nonmarital, 72
    overview, 16–18
    parental disapproval of, 66, 119
    sequence of events, 16–17
"Sexual awakening," 13–14
Sexual coercion, 83–91
Sexual entanglement, avoiding, 125–27
Sexual intercourse
    bonding during, 65–66, 74–75
    normal behavior, 72–73, 111
    oxytocin and, 33–35

Sexual manipulation, 88–91
Sexually transmitted diseases (STDs), 15, 36, 77, 80, 97, 121
Short-term sexual relationships, 12, 38–39, 56, 63, 108–9, 115
Significant others, 100–101
Statistics
    on contraceptives, 82–83
    depression/suicide attempts, 77
    multiple sexual partners, 58, 74
    sex outside of marriage, 73, 98–99
    STD cases, American, 80
    on unmarried teen mothers, 81–82
STDs (sexually transmitted diseases), 15, 36, 77, 80, 97, 121
Suicide attempts, 19, 77
Support cells, 25
Synapses, 26–29, 43, 51, 64
Syphilis, 80

Testosterone, 14, 19, 42
Trust, 36–37

Vaccines, 12
Values, 117, 126
Vasopressin, 39–41, 43, 44, 63–64, 108
Viral sexually transmitted diseases, 80
Virginity, 71, 123

TheMedicalInstitute

This book is the product of research conducted at the Medical Institute for Sexual Health.

To learn more about issues involving sexual health, logon to www.medinstitute.org or dial 800-892-9484.

The Medical Institute for Sexual Health (MI) is a nonprofit (501(c)3) medical, educational, and research organization. MI was founded to confront the global epidemics of teen pregnancy and sexually transmitted infections (STIs). MI identifies and evaluates scientific information on sexual health and promotes healthy sexual decisions and behaviors by communicating credible scientific information.

NEW RESEARCH ON WHAT AMERICA'S SEXUAL CULTURE DOES TO YOUNG WOMEN

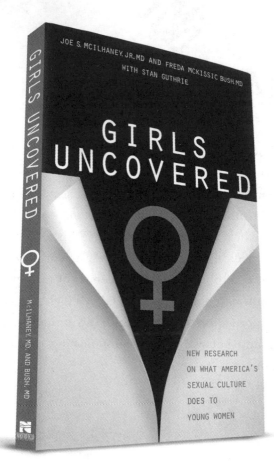

Obstetricians Joe McIlhaney and Freda Bush reveal the harrowing realities of prevalent sexual behaviors and attitudes in America and their psychological, social, and physical effects on young women. *Girls Uncovered* also provides fundamental wisdom to help parents, counselors, and church leaders guide young girls safely through the dangers.

978-0-8024-6298-5 | also available as an eBook